This book is
dedicated to the
legacy of
Nelson Rolihlahla
Mandela . . .

"OUR MADIBA"

To
Our Dave & Vicky
1 Sept. 2018

Thank You For Your Trains

From. Tommy & Pat
Solomons

Tafelberg,
an imprint of NB Publishers, a division of Media24 Boeke (Pty) Ltd,
40 Heerengracht, Cape Town, South Africa
PO Box 6525, Roggebaai, 8012, South Africa
www.tafelberg.com

Cover design: Michiel Botha
Book design: Nazli Jacobs
E-book design: Nazli Jacobs

Proofreading: Carel Cronje, Erna du Toit
Printed and bound by Interpak Books, Pietermaritzburg

Product group from well-managed forests and
other controlled sources.

FSC
www.fsc.org
MENGSEL
Papier van
verantwoordelike
bronne
FSC® C105735

First edition, fist impression 2014
ISBN: 978-0-624-06635-4
Epub edition: 978-0-624-06636-1
Mobi edition: 978-0-624-06637-8

# CONTENTS

# INTRO-DUCTION

Meeting Nelson Mandela simply took your breath 7 away. Ask anyone who was privileged to shake his hand. Ask the same person, however, what exactly it was about him that was so awe-inspiring, and they will find it hard to pinpoint one thing. His kind eyes, his broad smile, his genuine interest in the person meeting him, his mischievousness, his physical presence are all mentioned from time to time. Still, in the end, everyone would mention the remarkable aura of Madiba, which left you without any doubt that you were in the presence of greatness.

I experienced his amazing presence for the first time in 1990, shortly after his release from prison. Not only did he leave me totally in awe of him, but his words and actions (which I describe later in this book) also changed my life. I joined the ANC, which was of course not that common for a white person, and certainly not for one who bore the surname "Verwoerd". This in turn led to my election as an ANC MP in 1994, followed by seven glorious years in parliament. With Madiba as President, it was an extraordinary honour to have been a part of one of the most remarkable transitions the world has ever seen. Over the years, I was privileged to be present at many occasions where I could observe Madiba's interaction with people from all walks of life.

Naturally, there was a never-ending stream of celebrities and other VIP's from around the globe who wanted to shake his hand and have a photograph with him appear in the press the next day. I was present during a small number of these meetings and, with a few exceptions, they were usually short, albeit warm engagements. Yet those were the meetings that made the TV news and front pages of newspapers around the world. It is now also these meetings, together with the story of his phenomenal global and local political accomplishments, that are the focus of most of the growing number of books about Madiba.

However, away from the cameras and spin-doctors, with no political gain to be made, Madiba was meeting hundreds of ordinary South Africans for no other reason than that he deeply cared about people. For him every individual mattered and it was during these meetings with ordinary people that his true greatness shone through. It demonstrated, amongst many other attributes, his kindness, compassion, humility, sense of humour, love for children, gratitude, leadership, charm, courage, capacity to forgive and ability never to take himself too seriously. It also affirmed his commitment to inclusiveness and equality.

I saw this "Madiba magic" at work numerous times and was frequently moved to tears. Because of the emotional impact of these meetings, I related some in "The Verwoerd who toyi-toyied" that was published in May 2013. Many people who read the book remarked on my "Mandela stories" and then proceeded to tell me about their meeting with Madiba. After a friend told me of a telephone call from Madiba on his child's birthday, I realised that it would be very sad if these stories were not collected and preserved. I also felt that there was no better way to honour Madiba's legacy than through the stories of the people he had loved so much. So the idea of this book was born.

I made it known through various media outlets that I was looking for stories and the stories started to flow in. They came from all over the country and a few from around the world. Some brought me to tears and others were very funny. The storytellers were from vastly different backgrounds – the only thing that tied them together was a meeting with this exceptional man and the deep impact it had on them. However, as the book took shape it gradually became clear that it was evolving into something more than a tribute to Madiba.

It became obvious to me that the stories of his (often surprising) meetings with ordinary people should serve as a guide of the values that humanity as a whole and we as individuals should strive to uphold. It is often said that Madiba represented the best of humanity and the stories confirm this. Of course this did not mean that he was a saint or without shortcomings, and he always readily admitted that. In fact it is his sense of "ordinariness" and humility – something that is deeply lacking in our world today – that shines through in many of the stories.

Of course Madiba was and will always be remembered as a leader and a politician. So at a time where there is a serious lack of leadership in the world, I hope that this book will also serve as an inspiration and guide to all leaders and especially political leaders.

There can be no doubt that if all political leaders were to adopt more of Madiba's values, and act more like him, the world would be a very different, and better place.

For these reasons I divided the stories into various short sections – each representing a value or characteristic that I think Madiba embodied. I am aware that there are many more values and characteristics that can be identified and that many of the stories can belong in more than one section. I do not have explanations between every section, nor do I have a conclusion, since I wanted the book and every story to speak for itself. I was also determined to keep this book out of the academic and political terrain and therefore did not allow any academic reflections or political statements as part of the stories. For this reason, I excluded all South African politicians.

I further made a decision to focus on the stories of ordinary people and not on those of VIPs or celebrities. I don't really like the concept of "ordinary" (or VIP for that matter) and it is contrary to everything Madiba stood for. Yet, I wanted to give a voice to the many people who would not otherwise have had any chance of having their stories published, and it is their voices that show the true greatness of Madiba. I made a few exceptions and included the stories of Archbishop Desmond Tutu (how can you have a book about Madiba and not have the Arch in it?), Francois Pienaar, Angelique Kidjo, former Irish president Mary McAleese, Pieter-Dirk Uys, Johnny Clegg, Morné du Plessis, Ahmed Kathrada and Gary Player. I am convinced that all of them would in any case object to being called a celebrity.

I want to thank those who wrote, texted or told me their stories. There would not be a book without these contributions. A special word of thanks goes to Paul Emsley for allowing us to use the image of his pencil sketch of Madiba for the cover. My thanks also to Annie de Beer and everyone at NB Publishers, who made it such a joy to work on this book. My agent, Paul Feldstein, deserves a special award for sticking with me and for all the support. My sincere gratitude goes to Philip Fourie for helping with the translations and saving me days of work. Thanks to my friend, Abraham le Roux, for all his advice and wisdom. A special and big thank you to Carl McCann (Total Produce), Hugh Flynn (ASL Aviation) and Chris Horn for their financial support. They made publishing this book possible.

Most importantly, my biggest thanks goes to Nelson Mandela, who changed my life as he did the lives of so many others. Tata Madiba, the world is a much poorer place without you. We miss you.

# CARING

"What counts in life is not the
mere fact that we have lived. It
is what difference we have made
to the lives of others that will
determine the significance of the
life we lead."

NELSON MANDELA

# AMANDA STRYDOM

　　　　I met Madiba in 2001 at the opening ceremony of the KKNK (Klein Karoo National Arts Festival). He opened the festival officially that year. I was one of a group of singers who had to sing the National Anthem after his speech. I will always remember how he, at the end of his speech (which he delivered in faultless Afrikaans), held the *Groot Verseboek* on high and said: "Afrikaans is free!"

After we had sung the anthem, the Navy band began to play "Mama Thembu's Wedding" and he began to dance his well-known "Madiba shuffle". I caught his eye and also began to dance. I couldn't stop myself from running through his security guards into his arms. All that I could utter was: "We love you" and he whispered in my ear: "I love you too".

After the festival I went to Durbanville where I had to perform for a week. I stayed in a guesthouse whose owners kept three Rottweilers. To keep a long story short: the dogs attacked me on the

Sunday morning. I had bites on my legs and chest and scratches on my face. I was treated in hospital and the story hit the newspapers the next day. Madiba read it – he supposedly read all the papers, including the Afrikaans ones.

The next moment I received a call from his assistant, Zelda la Grange, who said that Madiba wanted to visit me because he was worried about me. I couldn't believe it.

He and his bodyguards arrived at the (new) guesthouse where we awaited him with koeksisters and peppermint tea (his order).

We sat down on a sofa and I was so nervous and astonished that I did not know what to say. He was calm and friendly and when we discovered that we both came from the Eastern Cape we started babbling like children. He told me that while he was still a court orderly, his salary was very small. At the end of the month he first paid for his lodging, then bought koeksisters, and what was left had to last him until the next salary cheque. I felt as if I was in the presence of some divinity – but also a loving grandfather. He made me feel as if I were the only and most important person in the room.

The photographer Johann van Tonder took photos of that day's meeting (he had also taken photos of the moment when I fell into Madiba's arms during the opening ceremony at the KKNK).

A few months later my husband Tony and I were invited to lunch with Madiba and his wife Graca Machel. There were just the four of us at the table – what a privilege. I still don't know what I had done to deserve it.

A few months later we were again invited to lunch – this time Joel Stransky and his wife were also invited. This time only Madiba was our host, because Mrs Machel could not be present. We laughed heartily when Madiba told Joel that he had almost given him a heart attack with the famous penalty kick at the end of the Rugby World Cup final in 1995. Madiba also warned me not to eat too much cheese, because it takes a long time for your heart and digestive system to assimilate it.

We were also invited to Madiba's 85th birthday celebrations – what un unforgettable evening. We shared the event with international guests like Princess Beatrix, King Willem Alexander, his wife Maxima, Bill and Hillary Clinton, Oprah Winfrey, Bono, Robert de Niro, Naomi Campbell, The Corrs – too many to mention.

What did Madiba teach me?

Forgiveness. This man endured and survived so much during his life, he could so easily have emerged from prison arrogant and bitter and power-hungry, but he did not. He addressed and treated **everybody** in our country with tenderness, love and dignity. He taught us what true greatness is.

Humility. In spite of his status as world icon, Mr Mandela was a truly humble person. It was not assumed. I will always remember how on the stage at Oudtshoorn he walked straight to the children, past the dignitaries, and talked for a long time with each one while they handed him their little presents. And at the meal at his house, how he waited for Tony and me in his sitting room and asked me: "Can I take your shawl?" He insisted that Tony sit in his chair, that chair in which he was often photographed. One felt the presence of a great man.

Unconditional love. Look at his life. What he believed, he lived. He assimilated and applied the hardship and the lessons that life taught him during his imprisonment, while the world anticipated a possible bloodbath in South Africa. It did not happen. His dedication and loyalty to the ANC was rock solid. During one of our meals he joked that, when he arrived at the heavenly gates, he would first ask where the ANC office was, so he could register.

There are few heroes in our planet's history who command so much respect, admiration and love from millions of people across the world as Madiba. I hope that in my clumsy way I could explain why. I experienced it firsthand.

# DOREEN SCOTT

I met Madiba the year he came out of Victor Verster prison, the very day after he was released, as I was one of the admin staff for Archbishop Tutu at Bishopscourt in Cape Town. We were all most fortunate to be introduced to him and his then wife, Winnie, and, as was the norm at the time, we all had tea together in the Archbishop's Lounge (Anglican Archbishop of Cape Town, The Most Rev Desmond Tutu). There must have been more than twenty-five people there that day. Madiba was such a gracious and well-mannered gentleman.

About three months later Madiba came back for a large political leaders' summit, which was again being held at the Archbishop's residence. As usual we all had tea together in the lounge. Mr Mandela caught my eye across the Library, smiled his brilliant smile, and made his way through the swathe of people to come and kiss me hello and ask me how I was doing. That really amazed and impressed me! He had met me ONCE, amongst a whole heap of new faces, and yet he remembered me, just one of several admin people and many new faces, and just after coming out of prison where he had been for about twenty-seven years! That is to me amazing grace – don't you think?

# JOHN CARLIN

Obviously, Nelson Mandela's greatness resides in his leadership, in his capacity to bend an entire nation to his will, uniting the most racially divided people on earth. Every politician alive, and those yet to be born, can and should draw lessons from his example. One lesson is that you can be the most effective of political leaders – in his case a global celebrity too – and at the same time be a decent and generous person. He shone bright for many reasons but most of all because of his integrity, because the coherence between what he said and what he did was diamond hard.

I have countless anecdotes to illustrate the point. I will focus on three, all involving journalists, a breed to which I belonged in South Africa during his epic years, between 1990 and 1995. These three incidents all took place in March and April 1994, an especially fraught time when not only was he criss-crossing the country on the election campaign trail, he was also battling away in negotiations to ensure South Africa's black and white right wing would not drown the entire enterprise for which he had sacrificed his life, as he would put it, "in blood".

Yet he found time one afternoon early in March to make a phone call to a woman who was of no political value to him whatsoever. She was British and did not have the vote. Her husband John Harrison, the BBC TV correspondent, had died that morning in a car crash. The call came in at her home in Johannesburg and a friend took it. The friend refused to believe at first that it really was Mandela. But it was and he spoke to Mrs Harrison for half an hour, offering her consolation, showing intimate solidarity with her by reminding her that his eldest son had died in similar circumstances when he was in prison.

About a month later the press pack accompanied Mandela, President F.W. de Klerk and the recalcitrant right wing Zulu leader, Mangosuthu Buthelezi, to a crisis summit at a lodge in the Kruger Park. The pressure was intense to get Buthelezi to drop his war-talk and take part in the elections. We had expected the meeting to be over and a press conference to be held at around 9 pm. But the leaders kept talking, and talking. They finally emerged after one in the morning. Mandela looked drained. He also had good reason to be dispirited. Buthelezi was not yet ready for turning. But, just before the press conference began, he realised there was another matter to which he ought to address his attention. He approached Debora Patta, a South African journalist and asked her, inquiring not just about her but about all the journalists present: "Debora, I am most concerned. Have you eaten?"

Just before the elections Buthelezi finally caved in. It was a huge moment, clearing the path to the fulfillment of Mandela's democratic dream. Another press conference was called, this time in Pretoria. Mandela finally had victory in sight yet he did not forget that something terribly sad had just happened. Deferring the announcement of the happy news, Mandela began, "First of all, let me extend my deepest sympathy to the family of Ken Oosterbroek." Oosterbroek was a photographer who had been shot dead in a crossfire in Thokoza township, on Johannesburg's eastern periphery, less than 24 hours earlier. "I sincerely hope," Mandela said, "that he will be the last journalist to die in our country as a result of the senseless violence."

Was Mandela being calculating in reaching out to the press in this way? Not in these instances. He already had all of us in his pocket by that point. Besides, in the case of Mrs Harrison, the phone call was not made public. I found out about it by chance some months later. Mandela was just being considerate, respectful and kind. He had integrity. He was who he said he was.

# ROY ANDERSON

Some months after he ceased to be president, I was invited to breakfast at Nelson Mandela's house in Houghton in Johannesburg.

No sooner had we sat down than he came to the point. He said he would like my company, Liberty, to build a school in Pietersburg (now Polokwane) for a community that was in need. I replied that Liberty had a foundation to which it contributed a percentage of its profits each year and that this would be a task more appropriate for the foundation.

But he made it quite clear that he was talking to me personally, and would like me to consider the options. The very next day I received a phone call from Mr Mandela inviting me to join him at Waterkloof Air Force Base with a view to flying to Pietersburg to visit the area and get to understand the needs of the community. When we arrived Mr Mandela was ushered into a stretch limousine and my colleague from Liberty and I were offered the second-best vehicle, which happened to be the local hearse. We drove to a high school that was in need of a primary school.

As we entered the building I began looking for the principal's office, but we walked right through the building into a quadrangle where we found the pupils, the teachers, the local MEC, headmen from the area and SABC television. Mr Mandela made one of his enjoyable speeches and sang along with the choir. Then he pointed to us saying: "You see those two gentlemen from Liberty? They are very rich. And now Mr. Andersen is going to tell you what he is going to do for you." Of course I told them that we would be building a school for them. Fortunately, it fitted into the corporate social investment budget.

I knew the pilot on the trip to Polokwane from the Border days. He told me: "Ja, General . . . tomorrow we're taking Mr. X and he will be paying for two schools . . . " It was amazing to see how effective Mr Mandela was in achieving his goals. The next time I saw him he said it was time to have another breakfast, but I was quick enough to reply that he had only to look at my waistline to realise that I had to be on a diet.

# SHIRLEY NAIDOO

Madiba always insisted that if we ever had any difficulty or something happening to us we should talk to him about it. Of course we did not like to bother him, but sometimes it happened inadvertently.

A few years after I started working for Madiba as housekeeper, the phone rang while I was with him in the lounge area. As was the practice, I answered, but the call was for me. It was my daughter who informed me that someone had scaled the wall at my house in Crawford the previous night and had stolen a bicycle. Madiba was always extremely inquisitive and mischievous. He would often ask you in the morning: "Darling what did you dream last night?" or "Do you have a special friend?" Of course we quickly learned not to tell him, because then he would mischievously tell everyone else or tease you. So when I put the phone down he wanted to know what it was about. I told him just briefly what had happened and assumed it was the end of the story. The next afternoon after lunch he instructed me to get his security and also lock up the house and let the rest of the staff go for the day. When I asked him why, he said: "I am going to your house to visit your family." I was totally taken aback and at first objected. "Madiba, it is your nap time," I said, "Zelda and Mrs. Machel would be annoyed with me," but nothing could change his mind. So off we went in the convoy, me sitting next to Madiba. I was so overwhelmed that when we got to Crawford, we went right past my house! I momentarily had actually forgotten where I had lived for years!

You can imagine how surprised people were when the cars with Madiba pulled up outside my house! It had happened so suddenly that I did not even have time to warn them. So Madiba sat down and drank water and spoke to everyone. Only then did I realise why he wanted to go to my house. He asked someone to show him the wall that the thieves had jumped over. He wanted to see how high the wall was. He was not impressed and after we left he got in touch with someone to put up a higher fence, so that my family would be safe.

# CHARM

"I take it you're a
student here?"
(to a forty
year old teacher)

NELSON MANDELA

# ANDIAH MYBURGH

It is Winter 2013 and I am working tranquilly on a painting of Madiba. According to the radio news he is in hospital; his condition critical but stable. My thoughts stray back to 2002 when I was in my mid-thirties and teaching at Sacred Heart College in Johannesburg. Mandla Mandela was a pupil there. It was of course a great occasion whenever his grandfather, Madiba, brought him to school. On that day I could see by the traffic congestion in the streets before and around the school that Mandela and his entourage were on the way. I mustered the courage to wait on the school veranda to greet our president myself. I saw the tall man approaching and suddenly started wondering what I should talk about to such an important person. Should I talk about young Mandla's music lessons? Or would Mr Mandela ask me about my political views? His calm smile immediately set me at ease. He put out his hand to greet me and said in his characteristic nasal tone: "I take it you're a student here?" What more could a woman of almost 40 ask than to be taken for a 16-year-old schoolgirl? The perfect compliment, and that from the president!

# JOHAN
# VAN ZYL

In August 1998 former president Nelson Mandela visited the editorial staff of "Die Burger" in Cape Town. This is how I recall that memorable day:

The stocky secret service men and their sniffer dogs arrived long before the lanky man gave his first shuffling step along the corridor.

"What do you call him?" a colleague asked when the staff, decorated with name tags on their chests, filed in to touch the robe of the head of state – the pious wish of innumerable people all over the world; people who knew that Madiba would never pass by an outstretched hand. "Do you call him Mister Mandela or Mister President? Do you have to genuflect? Can you ask him for his autograph? Will he remember my name?" Someone snarled: "Get real, the man mos meets flippen thousands of people!"

While we lined up on one side of the corridor as instructed, the nimble photographer Roger Sedres was threatened with capital punishment if he failed to capture every magic moment on film.

In the midst of the badinage Nelson Rolihlahla Mandela suddenly appeared. "Hello! How are you?" he asked with every handshake, and even before the (mostly) faltering "Fine and you, Mr. President?" continued with "Oh, very good!" As a diligent newspaper reader he would occasionally recognize the name of a reporter and generously dispense congratulations.

Guided by the editor at that time, Ebbe Dommisse, he shook the hand of Sonja Loots next to me, and was informed that she was one of the young staff members who had already published a book. "Oh, very good!"

And then, at last, his outstretched hand closed firmly over mine. In the eyes of the lanky man with the brown print shirt I saw unshakable convictions and the peace of freedom shining. The **real** Mandela, I thought while my heart drummed against the Bitterkomix T-shirt on which the president à la Superman streaked through the air with clenched fist. This I had donned under my shirt for a little private amusement.

Sonja looked at her palms. "Yes", she said laughingly, "probably nobody will be washing their hands tonight." We sauntered red-faced towards colleagues who were still waiting their turn further along the row, but suddenly the president was again shaking the hand of a (very willing) Sonja. Humiliation! "Hello! How are you? Oh, very good," he greeted her. When he stretched out his arm towards me for a second time, the editor leant forward confidingly and whispered that these two had already had their turn.

In December of the same year the domestic worker was waiting for her Christmas bonus after completing her daily task, and frowning at a photo in her hand. "I just wanted to know . . . " she said and held out the photo that she had found in a forgotten brown envelope on the piano, "where you can have such photos taken beside the Mandela mannequin? That really looks like Mandela standing next to you".

Two months later a friend from overseas also discovered the photo where it was still gathering dust on the piano lid. "You lucky beggar", she said, reiterating the almost consuming desire to touch the president's robe, and described articles on the internet by people relating how they had shaken the president's hand. All this she said with her fingers caressing the Bitterkomix Madibaman T-shirt which she had bought as consolation.

I am one of the favoured ones who **did** have the chance. When I look at the photo (thanks, Roger!) I remember the day that Mandela shook my hand. Twice.

It **was** him, I promise, the **real** Mandela.

# KABELO
# LEBOEA

Before the first elections, around 1992/3, I was at the Johannesburg Civic Theatre where Randy Crawford was playing.

During intermission a group of us was downstairs, having a few drinks and networking. This group was made up of the Dolly Rathebes and other icons of our country . . . all women; I was the only male. Suddenly Mandela, who was at the concert, appeared and walked towards us. He greeted all the ladies and then it was my turn . . .

He said something like: "Son, how do you do?" Instead of a response as would be expected, I was immediately sobered and brought to my senses, as if I had been very intoxicated. I guess it dawned on me then that I was in a sacred space with the main man himself. I can still feel the aura of his presence.

I was speechless and just managed to nod my head in admiration. It felt as if I was not supposed to speak to him. Madiba, on the other hand, looked like he understood where I was coming from. Of course, with his royal background, he would have understood protocol.

The next day at the Rand Water Board Central Depot and Head Office where I worked, everybody including the CEO got to hear about my achievement of seeing and being greeted by Nelson Mandela himself. I was the doyen of the company and my colleagues envied **me**! It felt like I should not have washed my hand at all to savour the moment forever.

What pleased me most was that as years went on, it became so difficult to reach and meet Madiba. I always tell people around me, especially my children, that I did not have pay a cent to see him and also that he came to greet me, instead of the other way.

Ijoo! Best moment of my life.

# MELANIE VERWOERD

In 2003 Madiba came to Ireland (where I was serving as South African Ambassador) to attend the Special Olympics. During his time in Dublin we dealt with a string of visitors, including Sir Anthony O'Reilly, Mohammed Ali, the Shrivers and Kennedys, Bono, the Edge, Arnold Schwarzenegger and Gerry Adams. One of the funniest meetings that took place was with the actor Pierce Brosnan. He was staying at the Four Seasons hotel, and after bumping into him in the lobby I offered to introduce him to Madiba. I knew that Madiba was on his way down to the lobby and asked Pierce to wait a few minutes while I went over to the lift to warn Zelda. As the door opened, I quickly told Zelda in Afrikaans that Pierce Brosnan was around the corner. Zelda turned to Madiba and said: "Madiba, Pierce Brosnan is out there to say a quick hello."

Madiba frowned and looked puzzled.

"Who?" he asked.

"Pierce Brosnan, the actor. He played James Bond in the movies," Zelda responded.

Madiba shook his head, clearly having no clue who she was talking about. It suddenly struck me that he had been in jail during the time all the Bond movies were made. I presumed Robben Island prisoners did not have movie nights, and since Madiba's release there would have been no time to catch up on almost three decades of films.

Zelda looked exasperated and said: "Madiba, we don't have time to explain, can you just greet him?"

Madiba nodded as he walked out of the lift. In the lobby I introduced Madiba to Pierce. Madiba looked at him, shook his hand and said warmly: "Ah, Mr Brosnan. It is a real honour to meet you at last!" Pierce was of course overwhelmed to meet Madiba – and none the wiser.

Later that night in the stadium, while waiting in the green room for Madiba's turn to go on stage, we were all watching the opening ceremony on television. When Pierce came on stage to the accompanying Bond music, the crowds went mad. Madiba turned to Cyril Ramaphosa, who had arrived a few days earlier from South Africa. "Hey, I met that fellow today! He must be famous with that amount of applause." Cyril looked at Madiba in astonishment for a few seconds before bursting into uncontrollable laughter.

# PAUL
# EMSLEY

During 2011 I began to think of the possibility of doing a portrait of Nelson Mandela. I had seen many portraits of him but most of them seemed to lack the necessary gravitas I felt he deserved. I knew that as he was by now advanced in years I should not waste any time. I tried various routes to gain permission but found it very difficult. Eventually after about eighteen months the project was approved after the intervention of Brundyn + Gonsalves Gallery and Anet Pienaar-Vosloo. There followed a period of correspondence about my intentions and the conditions under which I would work. Eventually I received an email from the Nelson Mandela Foundation to say that I had been granted a short photographic session a few days later in Johannesburg.

I hastily booked a ticket from London and prepared all my equipment. I was warned that I was taking a risk as due to his age Mr Mandela sometimes felt unable to come to his office for an appointment. At the Nelson Mandela Foundation offices I received a courteous welcome and I was eventually taken to a room next to his office to await Mr Mandela's arrival. As I was waiting I had the rare privilege of hearing through the open door Mr Mandela, his wife and staff members singing happy birthday to Archbishop Tutu over the telephone.

I was introduced to Mr Mandela in his office and found him most welcoming and friendly. As I was preparing my equipment we chatted briefly. To begin with I tried to be cautiously objective being mindful of the mythology surrounding the man. However, I soon experienced his legendary charisma, presence and dignity. I had a strong sense of benign authority. I could well imagine the enormous effect he would have on those with whom he engaged in politics and matters of state.

When I was introduced to him he said to me: "Hoe gaan dit met jou?" (How are you?) A staff member quickly explained to him that I was "from London" and thus did not speak Afrikaans. I didn't wish to complicate things by saying that Madiba was in fact correct. Although I live in England my wife is Afrikaans-speaking and our home language remains largely Afrikaans.

As I began taking photographs Mr Mandela continued to smile with great charm. I had to ask him politely whether he would please not smile so engagingly, as my intention was to produce rather a serious image. It was interesting to observe how hard he needed to concentrate in order to achieve this. As his smile gradually began to fade I continued to take photographs and it was these images with just the hint of a smile remaining, which I used for the final portrait.

I was using a new camera which I didn't yet fully understand. As we talked I found him so compelling that I did not notice that the camera was clicking away on it's own. As a result I now have a wonderful series of photographs of Mr Mandela's feet.

The initial intention was that the portrait would be donated to a museum, but before this could happen the Nelson Mandela Foundation asked me to consider donating it to them. This I have done and I have permission to do a second version for a museum.

# SHAUN
# JOHNSON

In Dublin years ago I was given a funny book called *Everyone's got a Bono story*. I immediately thought that back home in South Africa there should be one called *Everyone's got a Madiba story*, so widely and affectingly did he touch everyone – great or humble – with whom he came into contact.

Everyone who ever met Nelson Mandela treasures that memory to this day. Having had the great privilege of working in close proximity to him as a journalist and editor, and then setting up his leadership development charity, The Mandela Rhodes Foundation, I am no exception. And so to one of **my** Mandela stories.

Setting up Foundations requires fundraising and from 2003 I began to travel the world in search of donors to support an endowment for the sustainability of the then-new Mandela Rhodes Scholarships. On one particular trip on which I accompanied Mr Mandela and his wife Graça Machel we needed, after a series of meetings in London, to get to Monte Carlo where the Mandela charity organisations were hosting an extremely swish gala fund-raising dinner jointly with Monaco's royalty (as well as celebrities including Morgan Freeman, Wyclef Jean, Jimmy Cliff and Bono). As was not unusual, Mr Mandela was flying commercial (British Airways, which was always very supportive during his travels) and so we headed off to the VIP holding room to wait for the flight to Nice.

For reasons I still do not understand but am forever grateful to BA for, Mr Mandela's party was boarded *before* the rest of the passengers. Mr Mandela, Mrs Machel and Mr Mandela's assistant Zelda la Grange were booked in the front of the small plane in 1a, 1b and 1c respectively. I was a row back with a couple of other colleagues, I think, but Zelda and I swopped seats because there were Foundation matters on which I needed to brief the Mandelas, so I was in 1c.

Picture the scene when the punters started to board. They get to the top of the stairs, show their boarding passes to the flight attendant, turn right and . . . walk slap bang into a beaming Nelson Mandela. Without missing a beat he says: "Welcome aboard! So good to see you. How are you?"

Deliriously happy chaos ensues as unbelieving passengers are courteously received by the most famous man in the world and told they are welcome to take pictures with him. From children to elderly ladies; all are smitten. The flight does not take off on time, or even close to on time. The Captain says he feels that given the reason for the delay no one will be seeking an apology or compensation. (Typically, Madiba is totally unfazed by the whole thing and when the tumult dies down turns his attention to the newspapers). And everyone had a Mandela story. When we landed Mr

Mandela and his party were offloaded first, much to the disappointment of his fellow travellers.

And me? Well, I couldn't resist keeping the three boarding passes: Mandela, Machel, Johnson . . . just in case there are those who don't believe my story.

# COMPASSION

"Our human compassion
binds us the one to the other –
not in pity or patronizingly,
but as human beings who
have learnt how to turn our
common suffering into hope
for the future."

NELSON MANDELA

# DESMOND TUTU

A few years after Madiba had stepped down as President I went to have lunch with him at his house in Houghton, Johannesburg. After lunch Madiba walked me to the door. As we got outside the front door, he called: "Driver, driver!" clearly looking for someone he assumed would be there to drive me back to my house in Soweto. I said: "No, no. I drive myself," and bid him goodbye. Madiba did not say anything, but a few days later I got a message that someone had agreed to contribute R5000 a month for a driver for me, so that I did not have to drive myself. On investigation it became clear that Madiba had phoned a businessman to ask him to do this, since he did not want me to drive on my own.

That just blows your mind, doesn't it? I mean, I know that there are many business people who have been a bit worried over the years to take a call from Madiba, because no one can say no to him. But to me it just shows his amazing care and compassion. And it is a compassion that is not just for show. Our conversation was very private and so was his conversation with the business person. It was not a publicity stunt or to look good. He did it out of a true place of care and compassion. And that is what he will be remembered for, by so many, for so long.

# JANE
# PAYNE

Nelson Mandela visited Nazareth House, run by the Sisters of Nazareth, on 26th November 2002. He was 84 years old at the time and had been visiting various children's charities around Cape Town. Mr Mandela was quite frail and was introduced to all the nuns. One of them, Sister Mary was the same age as he was and the two of them walked up the steps to the Children's Centre, where the Sisters care for abandoned, orphaned and terminally ill children.

Sister Mary and Mr Mandela sat down side by side and they held each other's hand throughout, whilst the children sang various songs for him. Sister Mary was so excited and told Mr Mandela that meeting him was a dream of a life-time come true. Her face was a picture of joy. It was so moving to see the two of them, both rather frail and old, who both had served their communities and at the age of 84 still cared about the plight of vulnerable children.

Throughout the visit Madiba was so interested in the children. But for me it is the image of Sister Mary and Mr Mandela, two wonderful, elderly, gracious people, a nun and a former president, sitting side by side holding hands, that I will never forget.

# JOHANN NELL

"Daddy, I think my arm is broken!"

A weak little boy's voice on the other end of the phone made me brake hard. I had just picked up my daughter at Eunice Girls' School when my phone rang. I made a quick U-turn in the street and drove back in the direction of Grey College where my son was at school.

"You have to come and get me quickly, please!"

I didn't know what was awaiting me when I arrived at the school to pick him up. He was sitting alone on a little stool in the secretary's office. Two frightened eyes looked anxiously at me, and a wax-white face called wordlessly: "Take me to hospital!"

We sped away, while he lay on the back seat of the car, with the one hand tightly clutching the other injured arm. "How did it happen?" I asked my son.

"A big boy ran straight into me while we were playing touchies in the Phys-Ed class. I hit the ground hard. I tried to push him away, but he fell on top of me while I was trying to check him with the other hand. It feels as if an elephant fell on my arm. I swear it's broken."

I peered in the rear-view mirror to try to see the arm, but was convinced that it was nothing serious. At most it might be a muscle sprain.

On arrival at Mediclinic we started down the long passage to Casualties. I walked in front, my son behind, with his sister next to him for moral support.

And now?

What's this?

In the corridor before Casualties an unusual bustle greeted us. Men in shiny suits were scurrying up and down. Some wore dark glasses. In between men were running to and fro carrying massive cameras; definitely photographers and film crews, guards, security men. Everybody coming towards us. The three of us moving upstream. A sea of faces in the opposite direction.

But we struggled forward, like Israelites through the Red Sea opening before us. Then at the end of the corridor we saw the man. The world-renowned figure.

Can it be him?

It must be him!

Nelson Mandela!

The next moment he was right in front of me and my two children. The three of us dumbstruck before the great man walking towards us. He with his typical Mandela shirt, the sincere smile round his mouth, the friendly eyes.

I gestured to my two sprouts to stand aside to let him pass. But then Zelda la Grange's familiar face appeared next to him as she took a step forward. She walked straight towards us and made a friendly gesture which said: "come and greet him, it's all right."

And there we three Bloemfonteiners stood before Nelson Mandela. It was as if all the other voices and bodies and cameras around us had disappeared. There were just the four of us. And he actually reached out his hand to greet us. First me: "Hello, how are you?" I was so taken aback that I could not find the right English words to reply. All I could stammer was "Good."

He pulled my daughter Mieke closer with his arm around her shoulders. And she embraced him with both arms around his waist, as if he were the grandfather of the whole world. They gave each other a big hug.

Then Madiba stretched out his hand to my son, Wijbren. I wanted to exclaim: "No, his arm may be broken!" But Wijbren manfully extended his left hand and greeted Mandela, who held a walking-stick in his right hand, with a firm grip. Cameras flashed around us. Blinding lights shone from all sides.

"What are you doing here?" Mandela asked me. "It's him," I said, pointing to my son. "His arm . . . may be broken," I stuttered. "Oh," the familiar voice said. "What did you do?" My son answered in perfect English: "We played touch-rugby, sir. And another big boy fell right on top of me. And my arm was in the way. It feels like it is broken."

"Oh, I hope it is not broken. You must be very careful if you play rugby," Mandela said and smiled warmly.

And as suddenly as he had appeared before us in the hospital corridor, he disappeared behind us, on his way to visit a friend (I can't remember the name) who was seriously ill in intensive care. Madiba had come all the way from Johannesburg to visit him.

And we were at the right place at the right moment. And we had become a part of history. Not just part of the history of South Africa, but of our own, and of my children's – something they will never forget.

We walked away totally overawed. The doctor on duty said that Wijbren's arm was not broken, only badly bruised. With a few pain-killers it would soon recover. And fortunately the hospital manager phoned me the next day to say that there were a few very nice photos of our historic moment with Mandela.

# KIM
# BIEHL

In 1998 my sister Molly and I were invited to attend a breakfast meeting prior to the Congressional Gold Medal ceremony in Washington. This followed the killing of our sister Amy Biehl at the end of her time as a Fullbright scholar in 1994 in Khayelitsha, Cape Town.

At the breakfast four years later, Molly and I were standing together, feeling a bit overwhelmed. Madiba came into the room and saw us. He said: "These are the sisters of Amy and I would like my picture with them." Of course, everyone had been waiting for him (and to take photos with him), as he was the honoured guest. But he walked straight past the likes of Ted Kennedy and other well-known and important people, straight for us. Molly and I were both shocked. I have the photo on my desk at work and I always enjoy seeing the huge smiles on all of our faces, with Madiba's being the biggest of all.

# MARIAN FINUCANE

My first contact with Nelson Mandela was indirect. My husband and I went to South Africa in 2001 and met Ahmed Kathrada. He took us to Robben Island and talked to us about the prisoners' lives on Robben Island. Something that stayed with me was when he told us that when things eased up a bit, the prisoners were allowed to watch films. The prison wardens would bring everyone in and it was only after all the prisoners were there and the lights went down that they would bring in Madiba. Of course, that just added to his mystique and allure for the prisoners.

I would meet this extraordinary man again when he was in Galway in Ireland in 2003 to receive an honorary doctorate from NCI Galway. I was to emcee the evening. Beforehand we were taken up to Mandela's room in the Radisson Hotel. I remember being overwhelmed by his tremendous compassion, his warmth, his humour and this unbelievable feeling that you were in the presence of greatness. Someone then mentioned that we were involved with HIV/AIDS orphans in South Africa. Mandela told us about having visited some HIV/AIDS positive children who were in a rondavel in the rural areas. These kids had been completely ostracized because of their HIV/AIDS status and the community was dead scared of them. This was at the height of the pandemic and everybody feared about the disease. A big crowd had gathered since Mandela was there and he went into the house.

He went in to talk to the children and to engage with them. When he came out of the rondawel the people moved back from him. He said that as a joke he ran at the crowd and the crowd dispersed with screams. It really struck me how he was able to take a very serious issue and humanize it.

Afterwards, we went down for dinner and it was my extraordinary honour to be at Mandela's table. Mandela went out of his way to be courteous and kept thanking me for what I did. At some point The Corrs started playing and he got up and danced . . . and the place went bananas.

Later, when he was leaving he went out with John and me. In his one hand he had a walking stick. With the other, he took my hand and leaned heavily on me . . . I just could not believe that I was walking with Nelson Mandela on my arm and **he** was leaning on **me**. It was one of the best nights of my life.

Having met hundreds if not thousands of high profile people, I can say that Mandela was the most inspirational man I have ever met. His ability to bring people along and make them actively forgive, whilst never losing his principles and to have this amazing moral authority will stay with me forever.

# MARK LUBNER

My Mandela story is interesting in so far as my experience led to the creation of an organisation that will continue the legacy of Mandela's love for children – and that will continue for generations to come.

Madiba had an exceptional ability to care personally about individual children. His call to me in January 2000, was indicative of his concern for one particular child, whom he had met two years prior. The young girl suffered from a facial paralysis condition known as Moebius syndrome.

Madiba had promised the six-year-old girl's mother that he would obtain a surgical intervention to help remedy the situation. He called, anticipating to speak to my father who was out of the country at that time. In his determined manner he co-opted my commitment to getting the job done, irrespective of whether I had the medical knowledge to do so. But this was the art of Madiba's ability to inspire, for he expected everyday citizens to do something more than they ordinarily would in order to make South Africa a better place for all.

My investigations determined that the skill was not available in South Africa to perform the necessary surgery and I had to use my international connections to bring in a team of foreign surgeons to the country to perform this surgery and whilst here to teach local surgeons how to perform this complex procedure. This was the foundation for the formation of the Smile Organisation responsible for affecting 1000 surgeries on children from disadvantaged backgrounds. Today this organisation operates permanently in eight hospitals across the country.

One of the more memorable experiences relates to this period with the many meetings I held in Madiba's home whilst developing the fundamental principles of the Smile Foundation. I would take my eight-year-old daughter with me to share the experience. Madiba would always offer us both a cup of tea, but he would also instruct my eight-year-old child to take minutes of our meeting, believing that no South African should sit idle while others worked to build a better future for our country.

He wrote my daughter Takara a note which she has to this day, advising her that he expected her to be one of the future leaders of our country and this has inspired her to actively pursue a career in Social Development, after already committing herself to many worthwhile causes.

Madiba's ability to care about one child inspired both myself and my family to commit our lives to improve the circumstances and change the lives of thousands more children in need. His ability to make us care about the true nature of the heart of children will ensure that his values are perpetuated for decades to come.

# MARY DAVIS

On Saturday 20 July 2002, the Special Olympics joined together with the Nelson Mandela Children's Fund to celebrate the former South African President's 84th birthday. The previous year Special Olympics global spokesperson and athlete, Loretta Claiborne, had travelled to South Africa to promote Special Olympics. Her trip started with a visit to Nelson Mandela's prison cell on Robben Island to light the Special Olympics "Flame of Hope" for South Arica. This began a special relationship between Special Olympics and Nelson Mandela and his Children's Fund and led to the collaborative celebration of his 84th birthday the following year. Mandela spoke at his birthday celebration about unifying all people and how **all** children should be treated and respected in society – perfectly articulating the values of the Special Olympics movement.

As CEO, I was privileged enough to meet Nelson Mandela myself when he travelled to Ireland for the 2003 Special Olympics

World Summer Games. I remember meeting him at the airport on his arrival and I was struck by his charisma and sense of fun. There were some Special Olympics athletes there to meet him and he immediately went straight to them and began to ask them about their sport, their training schedule and wished them luck in the Games. I was inspired by his total belief in equality and his fight against injustice.

I was privileged to stand beside him on the podium as he made his speech to declare the 2003 Special Olympics Summer Games officially open. I was honoured to be there as he inspired the nation and the world with his words of hope, overcoming adversity and breaking through barriers and his message of dignity and respect. The speech he made at the Opening Ceremony and his interaction with the Special Olympics athletes at Dublin airport really high-lighted for me what a truly inspirational leader he was and the depth of his compassion for his fellow man. He showed a great understanding of humanity and looked beyond any differences to the unifying qualities within all of us.

# MEREDITH CARLSON DALY

Nelson Mandela's iconic smile – that broad, generous grin – is forever embedded in my mind, a memory I can pluck like a familiar hand-on-your-shoulder, offering comfort during this tremendous loss. I had the good fortune to meet Mr Mandela in 1994 in my homeland of South Africa, days before the historic elections. The journey leading to that meeting was a long one, a circle, a return to my childhood.

In the 1960s, as a young girl growing up in Johannesburg, the daughter of white, Jewish, anti-Apartheid activist parents, I witnessed the separation and hatred that defined Apartheid in daily life. My parents, Joel and Jeanette Carlson, taught by example: My mother was an active leader in the all-white women's anti-Apartheid group, The Black Sash. My father, who died in 2001, was a civil rights lawyer in a country without civil rights. He attended law school with Nelson Mandela, represented him on a few occasions and was a longtime lawyer for his former wife Winnie Mandela.

It was that 1994 moment with Nelson Mandela – and his brief words with my father that remain with me, a testament to Mandela's gift. Nelson Mandela's legacy of forgiveness, acceptance, dignity and determination was demonstrated in large and small ways. As President Obama said upon Mr Mandela's passing, the man they called Madiba set an example to make decisions "guided not by hate but by love, to never discount the difference that one person can make." My father and I were very fortunate to be the recipients of this tremendous gift in a deeply personal way.

My memories of South Africa are those of a child afraid and scared for how those living apart from us by night, but serving us our morning tea, would survive. I remember asking my parents lots of questions about the "kwela-kwela trucks," the police vehicles

that rounded up black men off the streets. I would see them pass by our house on 13 African Street in Johannesburg. At a young age I worried about those men – gardeners, cooks and cleaners – whom we were taught to hate, to rule, to subject and subvert. How would they endure after the kwela trucks had collected them and rolled down the heavy door, shutting them from sight and sound? I knew early on to fear and mistrust the police. They were those unfriendly officers who walked through our house after my father's car was firebombed in the night.

In 1971 my parents were planning something ominous. I was only eight, but I saw by the way they walked together in the evenings, huddled conspiratorially, talking quietly so they wouldn't be heard by the security police, who had planted listening devices throughout our house on that morning when they came to inspect the car bomb. It was understood in the activist community that conversations were recorded and monitored by police.

The South African government-run newspapers labeled my father a "terrorist lawyer." My father had unraveled the government's migrant labor system, won a pivotal case for 37 Namibian prisoners fighting for their country's independence. He had won the release of numerous woman prisoners, including Winnie Mandela. He had stirred the support of American President John F. Kennedy. Officials revoked his passport, forcing him to flee illegally. I remember the day he left without us. I watched him step through the airport security gate, his six-foot tall frame, his once flame-red hair a glistening silver, his green eyes never looked back to see a little girl, her hands cupped against the glass, eyes peeled for signs of danger. His broad shoulders carried so much as he stepped alone out of the country, forever.

Though my mother and siblings joined him weeks later, it seemed like months to me. We lived in New York City briefly with another exiled South African family, but my father never felt united. The life that followed was filled with the self-imposed remorse and regret of a survivor. He never forgave himself for fleeing or accepted that his decision was the right one at the time.

In 1994, more than two decades later, South Africa held its first democratic election. I was a reporter for The Hartford Courant, the largest newspaper in Connecticut, which sent me back to write our family's story, the story of an exile, returning for the first time. My father resisted my requests, anxious that my reporting would reveal his deepest fear: that fleeing his homeland was a cowardly act and that by leaving his practice and passion, he had relinquished his place in history. Yet he was torn. He wanted to vote in his country's first free elections and see some of his former clients ascend to leadership roles. He talked to former colleagues at the

United Nations, where he worked when he first arrived, and secured a position as a United Nations election observer.

My mother had no interest in returning, even briefly. "I put that part of my life behind me, happily," she said in explaining her decision years later. "It was so disgusting to live in that kind of environment where people were treated so badly. I had no intention of revisiting that."

In Cape Town where we were staying with my aunt, she mentioned that Mr Mandela would be speaking at her synagogue after morning prayers. After all, there were members of the Jewish community, such as my dad, who had supported him long before it was a popular position. The two of us walked together to services and I could feel his tension. He was sure no one would remember his contributions, or worse, would scorn him for abandoning his country.

Chief Rabbi C. Harris spoke of Robben Island and raised the question many had been thinking since Mr Mandela's release: How could he have survived 27 years in prison for the "crime" of wanting a political voice and leave without any bitterness? Mr Mandela, speaking in a raspy voice from a leftover cold, thanked the congregants for their commitment to their country, for their faith in his leadership. Afterwards, he held a private reception.

Perhaps because I had spent a lifetime growing up under my father's pall of doubt, I was stunned by Mr Mandela's gracious greeting of my father. As we neared the crowd of well-wishers, Mr Mandela noticed my father and extended his arms. He flashed that radiant smile, his eyes narrowing, almost closed, showing no judgment, no reckoning. My father approached him and grabbed his hands in a firm handshake. Still cupping my father's two hands in his own, Mr Mandela pulled him in close and uttered the words that have carried me through the years, lifting all doubt: "Joel, you got out in time," he said, in a confident, measured voice. "You did well. They would have got you."

How did he know that these words would be the balm to my father's burden, and my own? My father shook and cried. I excitedly tugged on his suit. He introduced me and I nervously scanned my brain for something profound to say when the words tumbled out: "I hope your cold gets better."

"Thank you," he said, nodding to me. "It will."

A week later, my father and I were seated among select invited guests at the inauguration of President Mandela. As he heard Mr Mandela again address the sacrifices made by many, including those who fled, my father hung his head and wiped his eyes.

"We dedicate this day to all the heroes and heroines in this country and the rest of the world who sacrificed in many ways and surrendered their lives so that we could be free," he said. To my father, who passed away from leukemia the day after Thanksgiving, 2001, and Mr Mandela, I pray that you rest in peace. I thank you for sacrificing so much so that those living may find peace, in many ways.

# MICHAEL ATTENBOROUGH

*Michael Attenborough on behalf of his father,*
*Sir Richard Attenborough:*

In 2004 we lost my sister and her daughter in the Boxing Day tsunami in Thailand. Shortly after the horrible event, my dad and mum received a handwritten card from Nelson Mandela that read: "I am so sorry I can not be with you, but know that I am hugging you." We were all so incredibly touched by the personal and deeply emotional nature of his words.

# CONSID-
# ERATION

"I learned that to
humiliate another person is
to make him suffer an
unnecessarily cruel fate.
Even as a boy, I defeated
my opponents without
dishonouring them"

NELSON MANDELA

# ADAM SMALL

Some time after Mandela became President, Prof. Jakes Gerwel (formerly a student of mine and later a good friend, and at that time Secretary-General in Mandela's Presidency) phoned us to say that Mandela would like my wife and myself to join him one evening for a private dinner at his official residence Genadendal near Cape Town. Of course we accepted. At dinner the evening, the usual shrimp cocktail was served as starter. I had phoned the housekeeper beforehand to tell her that I was a vegetarian, but it must have slipped her mind. I quietly sent back the starter. Soon a fruity alternative arrived for me! Mandela certainly noticed the incident, but glossed it over graciously.

On a later occasion Mandela sent a message, asking whether Rosalie and I cared to come, as part of his company, to Genadendal (this time the real Boland town near Greyton) where he was paying a visit. The day went off well. I found myself again at table with him. A breyani had been prepared. Perhaps, culturally speaking, this was not Mandela's preferred food. However, he took things in his stride, without fuss.

# AHMED
# KATHRADA

One of my most inspiring memories of Madiba is when we landed on Robben Island and we had to change into prison clothes. Coloured and Indian prisoners were given long trousers but Africans, in that bitterly cold winter of 1964, had to wear short trousers. They were not allowed bread, and their meat and fish and sugar were less than ours. Mandela was called in by the authorities and offered the same clothing and same diet as ours, and exemption from work. He refused.

# JAKES GERWEL

Once we were on a state visit in a very old country, staying in a very sophisticated place, when Madiba called me on the telephone late at night. He said: "Jakes, please come over here."

When I got to his bedroom, he showed me that there were some small insects emerging from the woodwork of the beautiful old bed and making their way onto the mattress. He asked me to lift the mattress from the frame and place it on the floor; and there he slept.

Early the next morning, he called me again. We picked up the mattress and placed it back on the frame because he did not want to embarrass his host.

# ZAPIRO (JONATHAN SHAPIRO)

In 2004 I had a surreal experience. I received a phone call from Prof. Somadoda Dikeni of the University of Transkei, before it became Walter Sisulu University. To my surprise he said that they had decided to award a honorary doctorate in literature to me. I was thrilled and asked to who else they were awarding doctorates. He mentioned some very important people **and** Nelson Mandela. I couldn't believe I was in the same group as Nelson Mandela. Shortly before the ceremony, I got a phone call, which explained that there had been a slight hitch. It was felt that Madiba should not accept any more doctorates in person, since he already had more than 300 at that stage. After the university protested, it was agreed that the university would come to Madiba's house and have the ceremony there. So I was told we had to get to Madiba's house quickly if we wanted to be part of his ceremony. My family and I drove through the day to Mtata and early the next morning to Qunu. I was put into a green academic gown and placed behind

Madiba during what turned out to be an extremely intimate event. There were probably no more than 150 people. As we filed in I asked the organisers whether I could perhaps give two cartoons to Madiba at some appropriate time. They suggested that I do it while he was on stage. Although I did not expect this, I was of course happy to do it. So after he received his doctorate, I was asked to come forward. I stepped out of the convocation and went to him. He was seated and knowing that he was getting frail, I did not want him to get up. But being as he always was, so respectful and polite to everyone, he got up slowly from the chair. I explained that I had two cartoons for him, which I hoped he would enjoy. The first one was about his retirement, depicting lots and lots of people holding him back while he is trying to get to his armchair, books and Perrier water. He laughed loudly and it was clear how much he loved it.

Then I showed him the other one. It was a cartoon about his wedding on his birthday in 1998 that was not supposed to have been happening. At the time it was even denied by his spokes-person, Parks Mankahlana. In the cartoon there is a big birthday cake, which looks like a wedding cake and all the staff members are winking at one another with a caption: "The world's worst kept secret". He roared with laughter about this one – clearly liking it even more.

Later in the day my family and I were privileged to be amongst the small group invited for tea at Madiba's house. Mrs. Machel was cutting some cake for everyone. My son Tevya, who was then 4 years old, could not understand why Madiba wasn't getting any cake. Mrs. Machel explained to Tevya that Madiba could not have any because of his strict diet. Tevya said rather firmly that he thought Madiba should get some cake. Mrs. Machel gave in and said: "Ok, I will cut him a piece." She gave the cake to Tevya, which he then brought over to Madiba, who was delighted, presumably that for once he got some cake. Madiba then felt moved to make one of his impromptu speeches. He again rose slowly from his chair and addressed his guests, still holding the plate with the uneaten slice of cake.

# SHIRLEY NAIDOO

Madiba was the most perfect employer I, as his housekeeper, could ever have wished for. He never treated us like staff – we were part of his family. He called none of us by our names when he spoke to us in private – only "darling". And we called him "Tata", because he was like a father to us all. He was always considerate and easy, even when things went wrong. One morning I went out early and cut some parsley in the garden to use as garnish with his breakfast. I am very particular with cleanliness and rinsed it thoroughly, or so I thought. Madiba sat down as usual for his breakfast, but after a little while he called for me. When I got to the dining room, he said gently: "Darling, look here, is there not something walking on my plate?" It was a tiny little insect. I nearly died with embarrassment, but he would not let me take the plate away and he was not annoyed at all – just amused. He gently moved the parsley to one side and continued eating, while keeping an eye on the insect.

But he was also strict and insisted on good manners with his own grandchildren. When they were visiting he would tell me in Afrikaans (since the kids did not understand Afrikaans) not to clear their plates away and that they had to take them to the kitchen themselves. He was adamant that he did not want them to be spoiled. So he would insist that I was not to be at the children's beck and call.

# COURAGE

"I learned that
courage was not the
absence of fear, but
the triumph over it.
The brave man is not he
who does not feel afraid,
but he who
conquers that fear."

NELSON MANDELA

# AHMED KATHRADA

Some of the qualities for which Madiba has been praised did not originate with him: they were ANC policy. Like reconciliation. But what distinguished him was his style. He had a style of doing things. What comes to mind immediately is the 1995 Rugby World Cup, and also his invitation to the wives and widows of the former apartheid presidents and prime ministers to tea. That is a matter of style.

Of his courage, one example will be sufficient. When we [the Rivonia trialists] were arrested, right from the beginning our lawyers, apart from what the police hammered into us, told us: "You are going to die." But Mandela told us that this was a political trial, not a legal trial, and we had certain responsibilities to the organisation, to our people and to the world at large, so we could not be apologetic.

He told us: "We know we are going to die." Of course we didn't debate that, because we all more or less knew.

But the way he handled it in his address to the court . . . We had all seen the address, and agreed with it. But when one of the defence advocates was shown it, he commented: "Look, you chaps are asking for the death sentence . . ." In the face of the expected death sentence Mandela defiantly reiterated his beliefs, for which ". . . if needs be, I am prepared to die." This was an example of courage.

# RICHARD STENGEL

I was once on this airplane flight down in Natal with Madiba. It was a prop plane. I think there were six seats in it and there were maybe four of us on the plane. As soon as he got on an airplane Madiba picked up a newspaper. He adored newspapers. He didn't have them for so many years and he reveled in the touch of them, and he read every stupid story. And so we were sitting on the airplane, the plane was up and he was reading his newspaper, and we were about, I don't know, halfway there . . . I was sitting right across from him and he pointed out the window . . . and I saw, to my great horror, that the propeller had stopped going around. Madiba said very, very calmly: "Richard, you might want to inform the pilot that the propeller isn't working." I said, "Yes, Madiba." I walked to the front of the plane, and the pilot was well aware of it and he said: "Go back and sit down. We've called the airport. They have the ambulances out there and they're going to coat the runway with foam or whatever they do."

I went back and I told Madiba that, and he just, in that very solemn way, mouth sort of down, listened and said: "Yes." And then picked up his newspaper and started reading. I was terrified, and the way I calmed myself was that I looked at him . . . like the prisoners on Robben Island must have looked at him when they felt scared, and he just looked as calm as could be.

The plane landed, no problem. He never changed his expression or anything like that. He put his newspaper down and as we got into the airport and had a moment alone, he turned to me and said: "Man, I was scared up there."

It was such a revelation because that's what courage is to me. Courage is not about not being scared. Courage is being terrified and not showing it.

So I was heartened. I was given courage by looking at him, because he was pretending not to be scared, and that's what he did for his whole life. I knew then that the more you pretend that you're not scared, the more not scared you become.

# EQUALITY

"I hate race discrimination
most intensely and in
all its manifestations. I
have fought it all during
my life; I fight it now,
and will do so until the
end of my days."

NELSON MANDELA

# ADAM SMALL

Shortly after Nelson Mandela became President, the British Queen, Elizabeth, visited Cape Town. A banquet was arranged for her. My wife Rosalie and I were invited. At a point during the evening, I wandered through the dining hall and came to the table where former President F. W. de Klerk, Mandela, and the British lady, sat next to each other. I shook hands with De Klerk and Mandela, whom I had met in the course of time. But the British lady gestured anxiously that she was not interested in such intimacy. The grim-faced woman need not have worried, I would not have tried doing so.

# AHMED KATHRADA

The other quality that stands out for me is Madiba's ability to relate to young people, to older people, to children, to monarchs, to peasants, to everybody. He was able to relate to people with equality and respect.

Barbara Hogan and I were invited by him to breakfast one day and we found him talking on the phone: "Yes, Elizabeth, no, Elizabeth, yes, Elizabeth." And when he finished I asked him who he'd been talking to. He said: "I was talking to the queen." So I said: "How can you address the Queen as 'Elizabeth'?" He said: "Well, she calls me 'Nelson'."

# MARLEEN
# POTGIETER

In November 2000 I was invited together with a group of committed South Africans to have dinner with Madiba. We were all giving presentations as to why we were committed to the country. During one of the presentations, a very young Phumzile Mlambo-Ngcuka, who was at President Mandela's side through-out our visit, whispered something in his ear. The speaker was asked to pause. Mandela apologised for the interruption. "Affairs of state," he said apologetically. "A situation in Egypt." An urgent discussion was to be had with an international head of state. A telephone was brought on a guilded tray to the President. In his jovial, booming voice, he spoke into the receiver. "Kofi, my old friend! How are you?" It turns out Kofi Annan had telephoned to discuss Egypt. The intimacy of the situation and the fact that we were at President Mandela's dinner table, sharing a meal with him, made it feel as though this type of conversation was just a normal run-of-the-mill dinner talk, commonplace. You had to pinch yourself to remind yourself that this was the head of the United Nations chatting away to the international icon that President Mandela was and asking his opinion about something that could affect world peace. It felt strange and surreal.

# TONY MEEHAN

I was the Sound and Vision Unit manager in Parliament and was privileged to be on that memorable day when Nelson Mandela first walked into the place where apartheid began and where he came triumphantly to overturn it and take South Africa forward to his and Desmond Tutu's Rainbow Nation.

During his presidency, I attended all the sessions of Parliament when Madiba was host to many world leaders. In July 1994 the first foreign head of state to visit the "new" South Africa was François Mitterand, then President of France.

For the staff of Parliament, these visits were fraught with many challenges to satisfy the whims of the visitors. Each brought a team of their experts, both technical and administrative, and would arrive a few weeks before the head of state's address to Parliament.

The French were the worst of the bunch. They were unhappy with most things and even got Parliament to hire lighting consultants as they were dissatisfied with the lighting in the National

Assembly Chamber. This, of course, was where their president was to deliver his speech. After additional lighting was added to the existing (and adequate) system, the French team was satisfied; and there would be no "shiny spot" on the bald head of their president.

We never received any special requests from our own president, or his staff. Having achieved a greatness beyond most people, this giant of ours was way above the "little" things of life.

I recall a day or two before one pending state visit when two of my technical staff and I were testing the sound system in the National Assembly Chamber. President Mandela and his accompanying bodyguards passed by the main entrance and, glancing into the chamber, he saw us at work. He immediately broke away from his bodyguards to come and greet us. In his usual smiling way, he shook our hands, asked what we were doing and wished us good luck with our endeavours.

Another memorable occasion for me was when President Mandela and Queen Elizabeth II walked through the corridors to the National Assembly Chamber where the queen was to address the House. The protocol for the Queen, of course, was that one should only respond if she spoke to you or offered her (gloved) hand. For anyone to reach out to Mr Mandela was commonplace. In fact, he was the one who would greet and reach out to all.

I have a photograph of Mr Mandela on the day he came to Parliament to bid farewell to the staff. I am standing directly behind the great Madiba.

Although this is a wonderful piece of memorabilia for those in the picture, it once again tells another story of our great hero.

If one looks carefully at this picture, you will notice that Mr

Mandela's hand is outstretched to take the hand of one of the staff members to his left.

In spite of some confusion, with those around the former president wanting to be photographed with him, he spotted the blind man and immediately reached out to him.

Another example of that which epitomised his life.

# WENDY
# STOFFELS

I was employed at the School of Government,
University of the Western Cape (uwc). The Norwegian Government had funded the completion of the School of Government building and the King and Queen of Norway were in Cape Town to announce the opening.

A diplomatic dinner function was organised for the King and Queen by the School of Government to take place at Tuynhuys, the Presidential Manor.

Senior staff including myself at uwc were invited to the function and prior to that we were briefed in detail of the protocol involved when meeting royalty that "was to be strictly observed". We were told, for example, to make sure that we arrive before the King and Queen, not to speak to them unless spoken to, not to make frivolous conversation, not to make any intimate body contact, not to commence eating before they have eaten, etc, etc.

My husband was Chairperson of the Black Business Initiative at the time, and was also invited. He had briefly met President Mandela on two previous occasions. Once at a function at the President Hotel called "The President Meets Business". The other happened as my husband wandered aimlessly down an office corridor on a visit to parliament for the first time. He came face to face with Mr Mandela walking toward him accompanied by two body-guards. Mr Mandela, he says, put out his hand as if they were old friends followed by his well-known, "how-are-you" greeting. As quick as he shook my husband's hand, he was gone leaving him to quietly reflect how surprisingly tall Mr Mandela was and his glossy, healthy-looking complexion.

The evening of the diplomatic dinner was an intimate affair, 10 tables of 10 were arranged with one cabinet minister allocated to each table.

The President, his daughter Zinzi, the King and Queen, and a few dignitaries were seated at the main table.

There were speeches and singing by a vibrant local school choir during which Madiba wandered casually onto the stage to join the choir and then broke into his Madiba jive. The members of the choir beamed in awe of his presence.

An announcement was later made that the President, King and Queen would be leaving the building and anyone wishing to join in for a "handshaking goodbye" could do so. As most of the people in the room had daily contact with the President, there was not much interest and a small queue gathered to take up the offer. I, of course, would not miss this opportunity.

President Mandela, his daughter, the King and Queen and two other dignitaries shook hands with the small group.

When our turn came, the President greeted my husband with

his proverbial "aaah, you again, and how-are-you?" As they shook hands, my husband jokingly remarked: "Mr President, if we meet again, then you will have to make me a cabinet minister." The President bellowed with laughter. The King and Queen of Norway smiled politely.

Then it was my turn. I greeted respectfully and shook the President's hand which he acknowledged warmly. He was much taller than I would have imagined, and he had this mischievous aura around him. I brazenly asked if I could "have a hug". He reached out without hesitation with this wayward glint in his eyes and we hugged tightly . . . me hugging tighter than he. I was overjoyed and beside myself. The surrounding bodyguards looked on perplexed but stood back.

I then moved over to the King who was smiling broadly. He looked at me and said: "So, what about me, do I not get a hug?" We then proceeded to hug and the Queen just burst into laughter. At that moment I thought: "Well, there goes the end of that strict protocol briefing I was told to adhere to."

The only regret is that it was not captured on camera, but it remains a moment that I will always treasure.

# EVERY PERSON MATTERS

"A fundamental concern
for others in our individual
and community lives would go
a long way in making the
world the better place we so
passionately dreamt of."

NELSON MANDELA

# ADAM SMALL

Mandela was, as I experienced him, quite approachable. During his stay at Genadendal, the presidential residence near Cape Town, I thought that my children should meet him. My daugher was still at university, and my son at school, and, from a perspective of national history, meeting Mandela would be interesting for them. I let his housekeeper know. She called back and said that he would gladly welcome them, so one afternoon we drove out to his residence, and he obligingly posed with us for pictures with the children.

Another example of the respect I developed for the man: My wife's name, Rosalie, is not so easy to pronounce correctly. But whenever, on occasion, we encountered each other, he would come to me and ask: 'Adam, how is Rosalie?' – always pronouncing her name quite correctly.

# ILAN ELKAIM

Soon after Mandela was released, a conference took place at the Harare Sheraton Hotel Conference Center to discuss the way forward for South Africa. At the same time and at the same venue, a meeting was held by a group of businessmen under the auspices of the US government to promote US investment in Zimbabwe. I was invited to give a talk on Bulawayo's potential in that regard.

When both meetings adjourned for lunch, we mingled with many famous politicians. I was standing near the late Joe Slovo and we commenced chatting. Mr Mandela then walked up to us and Slovo introduced me to him. Mandela asked me why I was at the conference, and on being told, asked if I spoke any indigenous languages. I answered him in SiNdebele and our conversation then continued in my SiNdebele and his Zulu (the two languages are very similar).

About three years later, my wife and I went to the movies one

evening at the Carlton Hotel complex in Johannesburg. Afterwards, while returning to our car, we saw Mr Mandela and his
entourage descending to the ground floor from the escalator. My
eyes met with Mandela's and he nodded. I certainly did not think
anything of this, but on getting off the escalator, he walked right
up to me, greeted me in Zulu and asked how I was doing and how
things were going in Bulawayo! I answered him, dumbfounded and
incredulous at his recognition of me after years had passed and
after having only engaged with him in Harare for a few minutes.

# LEILA GIBSON

In October 1998, I was travelling with a friend of mine by plane in the Northern Cape and landed at the Springbok airport for refuelling.

While we were there, we got word that Madiba was coming into the town to open a new school and we decided to wait so that we might get a glimpse of him.

When his small private plane arrived and he emerged behind his security detail and walked down the stairs, a small gathering of about 50 people had crowded around to see him or meet him.

He waved and then slowly went through the crowd greeting various people with a hello and a handshake and a great big smile.

I was very careful not to crowd him too much and not wanting to encroach on his space, I stayed at the back of the group of people and just watched.

After he had greeted quite a few members of the group, his eyes scanned the people and fell on me at the back of the gathering.

He walked directly up to me and asked: "Have I greeted you yet?" I said: "No, not yet, sir." He took my hand and held my shoulder, looked into my eyes and said hello. He then asked if I would like a photo taken with him, which I gratefully and gracefully accepted. He found someone with a camera in the gathering, put his arm around my shoulder and asked the gentleman to take a photo of us.

The thing that stood out most for me in my personal interaction with Madiba, and in my observation of the way he was with each person he contacted that day, was the immense granting of 'being' he gave to each individual he encountered. For that moment he engaged with you, you were the **only** person his attention was with, which of course made you feel extremely special and acknowledged. I truly got the sense of his great, great heart, his true compassion for his fellow human beings and the real essence of his gentle, expansive being.

What an unexpected privilege and a memory that I will treasure forever. A truly great soul!

# MARIDA FITZPATRICK

I was still a young journalist with *Beeld* when the photographer Felix Dlangamandla and I were ordered to go to ex-President Nelson Mandela's house on his farm near Modimolle (then Nylstroom). I had braces on my teeth and was ashamed to meet him like that.

When we arrived, Felix and I were both soaked with perspiration after three hours in the hired car without air conditioning. We met Mr Mandela briefly at the front door of the stylish farmhouse. He was very charming. The moment was so overwhelming that I almost bowed when I shook his hand. I tried not to smile so broadly that he would see my braces, but it happened anyway.

He had not been the country's president for many years, but I called him "Mister President" anyway, because anything else would not have sounded right. He was taller than I thought, and it seemed to me that his eyes had a blue tint, which surprised me.

We were with him for only a short time, but I remember how

cordial and warm he was, how much he laughed in that short period of time. From nervousness my ears were ringing, and afterwards I could remember very little of what was said. I think he asked in Afrikaans where I came from. "Secunda, Mister President," I replied, and he smiled as if he knew the town and me.

And suddenly I was not ashamed of my braces any longer.

# MARK SCHELL

My grandmother, Grace Schell, turned 90 five years ago. She is still very much alive and kicking and still Mr Mandela's biggest fan. When she turned 90 years old the local newspaper interviewed her and asked her what her biggest desire was at her age. She told the reporter that she visited Robben Island on a regular basis in her younger days, due to a family member being a prison warden. There she got to know of Mr Mandela and her admiration for him started. She said that her dream was to meet Nelson Mandela.

Someone who had read the article in the newspaper knew Mr Mandela's assistant. They called Zelda la Grange and told her my grandmother's wish. She in turn spoke to Mr Mandela who said he would like to meet her in person and invited her to travel from Cape Town to Johannesburg to meet him. My grandmother being 90 years of age would have found it very difficult to travel on her own and my brother, Dean, assisted her during the flight from

Cape Town to Johannesburg where I collected them. The next day my grandmother, brother, wife and myself left early to go and visit Mr Mandela at the offices of the Nelson Mandela Children's Fund. On arrival we were warmly met by a staff member and ushered to his office.

Mr Mandela came out into the waiting room to greet us and then invited us into his office. He spent about an hour talking to my grandmother about the old days. My grandmother was brought to tears a few times reminiscing about the old days and the visits she had to Robben Island. I was really taken aback by the height and the strength of presence of Mr Mandela and will always remember this visit. But what I will remember most is the joy that I saw in my grandmother's eyes.

# MARY McALEESE

During my fourteen years as President of Ireland, I met Nelson Mandela on quite a few occasions in places as diverse as Madrid, Mozambique and Croke Park, Dublin. Each meeting had a different character and purpose but it is the Croke Park encounter that stays most vividly in my memory. The occasion was the opening night of the Special Olympics World Summer Games in 2003. Ireland was hosting the games, the first time they had been held outside of the United States. The atmosphere was one of undiluted pure fun. Inclusiveness, camaraderie, transcending the odds, overcoming gargantuan obstacles, these were the leitmotifs of the Games and of course they resonated deeply with the life of our guest of honour, Nelson Mandela. My escort on the night was one Diarmuid O'Connell, from Valentia Island County Kerry, son of the legendary Gaelic footballer Mick O'Connell. Diarmuid has Downs Syndrome and is a great man for the big occasion. It was arranged that I would have a private meeting with

Nelson Mandela in one of the private rooms off the stadium. Diarmuid came with me. The end result was Diarmuid had a long private meeting with Nelson Mandela and I sat and listened as they chewed the cud like two old mates. No-one was going to hurry Nelson Mandela away from this important encounter and several times press officers and protocol personnel signalled that time was up. Oh no it wasn't. Diarmuid had another important point to make about the greatness of Kerry above all other counties and Mandela was not to be let out of that room without the full list of Kerry's All-Ireland Senior Football Championship wins beginning in 1903. We had just got to 1980 when the panic-stricken organisers managed to get their message across. Mandela gave Diarmuid a big hug and Diarmuid gave Mandela a big hug. Later when we got back home and Diarmuid's parents asked him how the night had gone and what famous people he had met, he replied with his customary humility. "I met Nelson Mandela and he told me that he was thrilled to meet me." And so he was.

# MELANIE VERWOERD

While he was president, I once travelled with Madiba from Waterkloof Military Airport outside Pretoria to the official residence. While we were driving it struck me that Madiba had only one security car in front and one behind, and that they kept to the speed limit. His security later explained that he insisted on abiding by all the laws of the country, including speed limits. It was still early morning in Pretoria, and traffic was fairly light. On street corners and at traffic lights, hawkers and newspaper sellers were setting up for a day of trade around fires to keep them warm. At every red light (of course there was no jumping of lights), Madiba would wind down his window and greet the traders, who, to the security's exasperation, would rush over to say hello – once they had got over the shock of meeting their beloved Madiba.

A few years later I had a similar experience with him in Dublin. On our way from the airport, Madiba and I were having an intense political conversation. But as we would pull up at traffic lights, people in cars next to us would recognise him. Time and again they would roll down their windows to say: "How's it going, Mandela? Welcome to Ireland." Madiba would politely reciprocate and, to his security's annoyance, roll down the window to say hello. "The Irish are very friendly," he would remark, before continuing with our conversation.

# PAUL WEINBERG

Like it did for millions throughout South Africa and the world, President FW de Klerk's announcement of the release of Nelson Mandela and the unbanning of political organisations took me completely by surprise. At the time I was part of Afrapix, a photographic collective, which I co-founded. Together with my colleagues, we had been covering the events, which we had been feeding to the alternative and mainstream media for a decade. In true collective style, a meeting was held and a decision (by consensus) was made that I should fly from Johannesburg to Cape Town to cover this historic moment.

My friend and colleague, Paul Grendon, in his beat up old Volksie, picked me up at the airport. We made it slowly but surely to the gates of Victor Verster prison. There were tiers of photographers and cameramen in position and waiting. Not surprisingly, we were met with a bit of hostility by the world's media who had descended on this location for one of the major stories of the 20th century and had been waiting for hours already. Grendon, I suppose, didn't help our cause. A serious documentary photographer, he came equipped with a Leica, no long lenses, flap jacket or the paraphernalia that at least on the surface could have given the appearance of a photojournalist. I sheepishly tried to find a spot and a relatively good vista. My initial position was behind a *Time* magazine correspondent and his partner. The wind kept blowing her long flowing hair and so obscuring my vision. "Do you mind moving slightly to the left?" I asked her at one point. "No, I won't!" she said, "I've been waiting here for eight hours." My response was immediate and I am not entirely sure where it came from, but it sounded well rehearsed. "Well, I and millions of others have been waiting all our lives." I then settled on a place which was more like a worm's eye view. At least I had a clear path to the gates.

After much anticipation and more waiting, Madiba and Winnie walked through the gates toward the media. I focused and pressed the shutter. Just as I did it, a group of comrades who were to my right, surged. My cameras, camera bag and I went flying. So my Madiba moment consisted of blue sky and telephone lines! To add further ignominy, I lost a lens in the fracas. Grendon and I then headed to the Grand Parade where I hoped to redeem myself. It was jammed tight and I began a long and difficult push towards the balcony of the City Hall where Madiba would later speak.

It was, as we know, another long wait. The driver got famously lost and the light began to fade. By the time Madiba appeared the sun was beginning to set and all I could do was point my long lens in the direction of the balcony knowing it would be a blurred failure, and so another missed historic moment. To rub more salt into my wounds, I was pickpocketed and lost R300 as well as my light meter. On that day my attempts to interact with history were a dismal and spectacular flop.

The next day at Archbishop Tutu's residence, Nelson Mandela appeared for his first press conference and portrait session. This time I was way ahead of time and to my surprise there was a very manageable group of photographers. I took what became his very first portrait post his imprisonment. Thankfully these images worked well and were used extensively by the media.

Caught up in the events that followed I joined the Mandela train to some extent as he connected with the South African public. On one occasion I was commissioned to do 'a day in the life' of Nelson Mandela. I shared the moment with a film crew who were exceptionally restricting and prevented me from using flash in low light situations. At one point as we walked along the corridor Madiba, remembering my name, turned to me and asked, "Are you related to my good friend Eli Weinberg?" I have been asked this question a thousand times in my life. I replied with the same answer: "Not directly but our forebears came from the same city, Riga in Latvia." "I see," Madiba said generously, but I knew my answer was not going to get me much closer to the great man.

However, when working for *Der Spiegel*, Paul Schumaker, the correspondent and I, had an opportunity to spend two hours interviewing Madiba over lunch. He was waiting for a lift that somehow was delayed and we had the amazing privilege to talk in depth about issues of the day and beyond. It was more like a conversation than an interview. He was relaxed and in top form. One got the distinct impression that Madiba knew when he was talking to you or allowing his photograph to be taken, that he was connecting with the world. The media were his direct artery to the world, which he so brilliantly managed throughout his life. It was also clear that you as an individual were as important to him as he was to us all.

My next significant moment was during the 1994 elections. I was the official photographer for the IEC (Independent Electoral Commission) and had special access to voting stations. Like his release, this 'moment' was what the world had been waiting for, Mandela voting for the first time. He had chosen Ohlange School at Inanda in Durban, the site of John Dube's grave. This time I was in position way ahead of time. I was nervous and took constant light readings to check that everything was in place. But as with every nervous moment there is often an unexpected drama. As he walked into the booth, an IEC commissioner from the US was walking next to him and had latched onto his elbow. Her eyes lit up as she saw me. "I want a photograph of Mandela and I," she kept badgering me. I had just a second or two to capture this moment. On either side of Mandela were Bantu Holomisa and Jacob Zuma. Then Madiba dropped his voting paper in the box. There were no raucous comrades to push me over and I got the moment! Nelson Mandela voting for the very first time in his life! I didn't get the commissioner next to him. The only part of her body is her hand on the right hand corner.

For months afterwards people would stop me in the street and say. "Don't I know you from somewhere?" As it turns out this was my five minutes of fame with an icon of the world. The TV cameras, which were there to film Madiba, also caught me taking the photographs. These images were broadcast to hundreds of millions of viewers. To be more accurate, it was mainly the image of my butt that was beamed across the world as I crouched down lower to frame the image of Madiba's moment in history – a very uneven contest!

# PEPE TOBIN

Quite a few years ago my husband, daughter and I attended the wedding of the late Arthur Chaskalson's son. We knew Madiba was coming, but when we got there he had not yet arrived. I and many other people were studying the seat-placing list. All of a sudden everyone just seemed to disappear and there was this hush – Madiba had arrived. The wedding started. Madiba walked down the aisle in the garden, but he stopped to talk to people, including my daughter. He asked her if she was getting married, to which she replied that she was only in matric (she is now 34). At a Jewish wedding there is a *chuppah* (a canopy under which the bride and groom stand). Madiba also sat under the chuppah and held the bride's veil the whole of the ceremony. It was very special for us and I am sure even more special for the couple. When the ceremony was finished he walked out and came specially to my daughter and said: "You must finish your education; there is nothing like an education." What amazed us was that, with all the people there, he remembered what my daughter had told him and came specially to tell her.

That memory of Madiba, will always live in our hearts. He was such a very special person.

# ROBERT SCHWARTZ

Our diamond and jewellery business in Johannesburg was founded in 1924 by my late father.

Over the years we have been manufacturing high class diamond and gold jewellery and from time to time branched out to other businesses.

At a certain time we were also the agents for Alfred Dunhill tobacco, pipes, humidors and smokers specialist items. Amongst the items we dealt with were Dunhill cigarette lighters. We gave exceptionally good after-sales service and employed a repairman, who unfortunately was not very well as he had diabetes. He was continually on medication and unfortunately he also consumed alcohol whilst on medication. This led to occasionally having bad fits with the result that he was from time to time off work and had to be hospitalised and dried out.

One of our other businesses was a company called Gun Runner (Pty) Ltd. Shortly after Nelson Mandela's release, I received a call from the Department of Home Affairs in Pretoria with a request that I meet with Mr. Nelson Mandela in our gun shop as Madiba wished to purchase firearms for his bodyguards to carry.

At the duly appointed time Madiba arrived in the chauffeur driven limousine from the Department of Home Affairs in Pretoria and entered our store. I immediately went downstairs, ushered him in, offered him tea and coffee. He really was one of the most charming and humble people I have ever met. He proceeded to ask our opinion as to what he should purchase and we duly assisted him and helped him with the purchase. He then offered to meet all the people in our building. It was a five-storey building, housing our various departments. I took him up in the elevator and introduced him to everybody in the building. You can just imagine how pleased everybody was to shake his hand and meet him. He took time and chatted to all of the people concerned.

One of the persons he spoke to was the cigarette lighter technician who had just returned from a drying out phase in hospital. His eyes were out on stalks while Madiba took time to talk to him; questioning him on his workshop and on how he repaired the cigarette lighters. He truly showed a real interest in all of the people who worked in our factories. It really was quite amazing to see the time and effort he put into it.

He then asked me if I would be so kind as to drive him back to Soweto, which I did, after helping him to take his fingerprints. (The police insisted on having fingerprints for gun purchases). He had arthritic hands and it was difficult for him to roll his fingers on the special finger print pad that the police had brought for me for the purpose. I then drove him home to his Soweto home where I met his wife Winnie.

He was most gracious and I spent at least three hours with him. It was a thorougly enchanting experience.

The following day I received a call from our lighter technician's family to say that he was back in hospital. I could not understand why, since he looked so well the previous day. The family member explained that he came home the previous night with some ridiculous story that he had met Nelson Mandela and that Madiba had sat and talked to him for twenty minutes while he showed Mandela how to repair cigarette lighters.

The family obviously assumed that he had been drinking again and was having another fit. So they shipped him straight back to hospital. I advised the family that the story was absolutely the truth and that they should immediately fetch him from the hospital.

We became well known to Madiba and whenever we went to a function where he was present, he would always walk up to us, shake our hands, speak to us and take the time and trouble to ask us how we were. At our store in the Sandton Sun Hotel one morning, he walked by and we had our young granddaughter with us. He came in, picked her up, spoke with her and took time with her. He said how nice it was to see us again and sent his best regards to everybody.

For us, he will remain the man of the century.

# SOLOMZI TONYELA

I met Madiba when I was still working in what was then called the Senate as a microphone operator between 1994 and 1995. Microphones were still operated manually then. I also used to operate the Members' register in the Senate.

The first time I met Madiba, it was just after a sitting of the Senate had adjourned. He was talking outside the Senate with the late Mr. Dullah Omar. I was on my way to lock up the microphones. While walking downstairs, I heard Madiba calling me. He said: "Good afternoon, son." I responded with a greeting and he asked me if I knew a man called Themba Tonyela. Then, before I could respond, he asked me if I knew a Douglas Tonyela.

He went on and asked if I knew a Thomas Tonyela. I finally responded and said those were my father's names. And he said: "Ewe, sasingamafafa amade kwedinin, oluhlobo lwakho." (Yes, we used to be very tall young men, your father and I, just like you.)

He never told me where they met and my father had never

talked about him. I later found out that they had gone to school together before Madiba entered active politics. He recognised me because he said I was the spitting image of my father.

After that he would greet me every time he saw me around Parliament. I also remember the visit by the Prime Minister of Singapore. I sing in the choir and the choir was performing at the event. When he saw us performing, Madiba came to join us, despite his bodyguards trying to caution him.

He greeted everyone in the choir with a nod, but when he saw me he said: "Mfondini, ukho kuyo yonke indawo, ukhona nalapha?" (Man, are you everywhere, you sing in the choir too?)

He then joined us in the choir, doing his famous Mandela jive. Afterwards, he asked if we had been given food. He always insisted that everyone be catered for and everyone be treated equally.

# USHA LALLOO

I never thought it would be possible: Word got around that Nelson Mandela was coming to Fordsburg to visit Amina Cachalia and family!

We lived on the second floor of what was called *Crown Heights*. The building has a lot of historical relevance as there was an active member of the ANC, Dr Jassat living on the fourth floor. We would often see the security police coming to arrest him in the early hours of the morning, from our flat windows. It was always a scary sight as he was a softly spoken man of a gentle nature. But he stood firm in his beliefs! He was an inspiration as we were afraid of the consequences of speaking out. Not far from the building was his office. It was located next to the UDF's offices on Bree Street and we would often see the likes of Mr Saloojee and other members going in to have secret meetings. Fordsburg was a central point for many of the activities that were conducted by the Indian community in Johannesburg.

Back to the fateful day of when Madiba visited Amina's house.

The back of Crown Heights faced Fordsburg Primary School and Amina Cachalia's house. From our second floor balcony we had a perfect vantage point to look into the garden terrace of her house where, as luck would have it, they were set to have tea. In anticipation of the visit, my son decided to 'play sick' and stay home. We knew why, and let him, because we knew this would be a historic moment.

We were on our toes the entire morning taking turns to see if the cars had arrived. The participants were myself, my housekeeper ( who remained with us for 28 years ) and my 'sick' son.

Finally, the entourage arrived to much fanfare. The school came to a halt and the occupants of the surrounding houses ran outside, waving with glee on their faces. It was a spectacle to see as the emotions were raw and full of excitement. The kids from the school were chanting, passersby waving and the housekeepers ululating. The excitement was beyond belief!

The bodyguards, dressed in black, secured the area and gave the go ahead for Madiba to exit the vehicle. With the Cachalia family waiting to welcome him, he smiled and waved in true Madiba style to the adoring people from the school, homes and building.

We got the first sense of his humility in greeting ordinary people as warmly as he would dignitaries. People were beside themselves as this was a moment so long anticipated.

Madiba and his delegation moved quickly into the house and the excitement slowly dissipated. However, we knew that the tea was to be held on the back terrace of which we had a good view. We remained glued and waited . . .

We first heard the iconic voice before we saw Madiba. Then we watched them having tea, while chatting and laughing.

Helen our housekeeper was transfixed and when Madiba finally got up to leave, she could not handle it any longer. So she shouted loudly: "Madiba!" He turned around slowly and looked up at myself, Helen and Ajay. Then he smiled broadly and waved.

Filled with a sense of pride that he had acknowledged us, we felt as if we were floating!

Needless to say, the story of our moments "with" Madiba lasted days, weeks, months, years.

# ZAPIRO (JONATHAN SHAPIRO)

In 1998 I was busy doing a cartoon on an ordinary working day when the phone rang, and my wife said it was the President's office. I thought it was intriguing and maybe they wanted one of the cartoons. I was working hard on something and was sitting with the phone in one hand, while drawing with the other. After a while a woman's voice came on the line and said: "Hold on for President Mandela." By then I was convinced it was one of my friends playing a prank and was trying to figure out who it could be. Then that familiar voice came on the line and said: "Hello, is that Zapiro?" I said hesitantly: "Yes?" He said: "This is President Mandela." I said: "It sounds like you, so it must be you," since I was by then totally thrown. Then he said: "I am very upset with you!" I went cold, thinking he might have taken some of my cartoons badly. So I said: "What have I done?" He then explained he had just read that he would no longer be able to see my cartoons every day when he was in Cape Town. There had been a report in *The Argus* that they would no longer be re-publishing my cartoons from *Sowetan*, since I had a new arrangement with the *Sunday Times*, which they regarded as opposition.

As it turned out Madiba loved seeing the cartoons when he was in Cape Town for parliament and now he could not see them any more and he was upset about that. So he got his office to contact me and got on the line to tell me that. I was overwhelmed and told him how much it meant to me that he enjoyed the cartoons and above all that he took the time to contact me in person. We had a short conversation and at the end I said: "I am even more touched that you got in touch, because you would have seen that in the last four years, since I met you, my cartoons have become more and more critical of the ANC and of government." He replied: "Oh, but that is your job!"

That is the single most important thing that has ever been said to me. Because it was Nelson Mandela of course, but also because he was the head of the government and the country that I operate in. Here was somebody who completely understood the need for critical media, satire and humour. He saw himself and his government being criticised in the cartoons and still acknowledged and supported the role that I was supposed to be playing.

# FORGIVENESS

"Forget the past."

"If you want to make peace
with your enemy, you have to
work with your enemy.
Then he becomes your partner."

NELSON MANDELA

# CHRISTO BRAND

After Mandela's release I resigned as a prison warden on Robben Island and became a civil servant while the new constitution was being drafted. One day Mandela flew into Cape Town by helicopter and entered the room where members of parliament were debating the new constitution.

Mandela went around the room shaking hands with parliamentarians, but when he saw me, who was distributing documents, he lifted his arms and warmly greeted me.

He immediately made a big announcement to everyone: "You know who this person is? This person was my warden, this person was my friend." I felt very humble and proud at that moment. After that when the parliamentarians went out for a group photo, Mandela insisted that I should also be in the photo. He said: "No, no. You must stand next to me, we belong together."

# MELANIE VERWOERD

About a year after his release, Madiba was invited to a private meeting with some progressive Afrikaners in Stellenbosch. The cocktail party was to be held at Jannie Momberg's house. Jannie, a former wine farmer, had joined the ANC and later became one of the senior whips in the new parliament. Jannie had invited myself and Wilhelm (my husband at the time) to attend. The meeting caused a stir in Stellenbosch. On the night, there were various members of the press present. Mandela, with his amazing charm, quickly put everyone at ease, and people started to talk to him. Being academics, they tended to keep their emotions under control and engage more intellectually.

We hung back, but at some point Oom Jannie spotted us. Never a very discreet diplomat, he pushed everyone away and pulled us closer, then introduced us to Mandela. The moment Mandela heard the surname, his eyes lit up. "Ah, I am so honoured to meet you," he said in a sincere, warm voice. My heart was racing. I had no doubt that we were in the presence of greatness. How could he be honoured to meet us – especially with the surname? After all, it was Wilhelm's grandfather, the architect of apartheid, the symbol of oppression, who had banned the ANC, and it was during his time as prime minister that Mandela had been incarcerated.

Wilhelm started to talk politics, and then tried to apologise for his family's role in Mandela's personal suffering.

But Madiba stopped him. "No," he said, "you only need to remember that with the surname you both bear, you have a voice. People will listen to you. So you have to think carefully what to do with that power." He paused for a moment, then said: "By the way, how is your grandmother?"

Slightly taken aback, Wilhelm explained that she was well, even at ninety-two, and, slightly embarrassed, admitted that she had moved to Orania, a whites-only enclave in the Northern Cape.

Mandela looked at us earnestly and said: "If she will not get angry at you, please send her my regards. Tell her from an old man that I am happy that she has reached such a great age."

By now I was shaking. What an extraordinary man: no bitterness, no anger. After twenty-seven years of being unfairly imprisoned, he did not seek revenge. In fact, the opposite: he sent his sincere regards to the wife of the man who was behind his incarceration!

# RORY STEYN

I have many memories from the five years that I was privileged to serve Madiba and it had a profound effect on (and changed) my thinking, behaviour and my worldview.

I think it started on Inauguration Day, May 10, 1994. Part of the celebrations on that momentous day was Madiba's attendance at a football match between South Africa and Zambia at Ellis Park. He arrived a little late because of the earlier festivities at the Union Buildings. With everyone wanting to congratulate him, he overran slightly. After the match he had to return to Pretoria for the lunch he was hosting for more than one hundred and fifty heads of state or government.

So after greeting the teams on the field at halftime (instead of before the match as is traditional), he got into his armoured car for the trip back to the waiting helicopter. But just as we were about to drive away, he got out of the armoured car without any explanation to the protection team. He then walked across the floor of the hall where the car was parked behind the President's Suite, straight towards a police colonel on the other side of the hall.

The colonel, in full uniform, was as confused as the rest of us and his eyes grew larger and larger as Madiba walked directly towards him. (This was a real old "polisie-kolonel" as we knew them in 1994. He was Afrikaans, in his mid-fifties, white, lots of 'miles on the dial' and had a lined face that had certainly been there and seen it all.)

Surrounded by about ten VIP protectors, Madiba put out his hand and said to the colonel: "Colonel, I just want you to know that today, you have become our police. I am now the president of South Africa, but I just want you to know that there is no more 'you' and 'us' and, from today, you are **our** police."

The hardened veteran started quietly crying and the tears ran down his lined face and dripped onto the polished parquet floor. Madiba just patted his shoulder and said: "It's okay, Colonel, I just wanted to tell you that," and then walked back to his car.

As someone born in 1963, I was probably the classic product of apartheid conditioning and that conditioning had been further enhanced by a police career that included service in the Security Branch. I can honestly say that the encounter I witnessed between Madiba and the colonel that day caused me to question all that I had accepted as "normal" and awakened a hope that perhaps black and white really could live together in South Africa. I started to believe that Mandela's espousing of the philosophy of non-racialism was not simply some form of ANC propaganda, the party line, but a genuine belief. A belief that I now know was honed and refined by the debate amongst the wonderful minds of the stalwarts imprisoned with Madiba and lots of reflection on how it would all work once democracy was realised.

My transfer from commanding the VIP Protection Unit in Johannesburg to the Presidential Protection Unit in Pretoria in January 1996 to become team leader of one of Madiba's protection teams, meant an agreement with my commanders that I would accompany him on a state visit to the UK in July that year. If the five years that I served Madiba were the best five years of my life, then the four days in London were the best four days of those five years. (I slept three nights at Buckingham Palace, for goodness' sake!)

However, shortly after our return from London, I was summoned by my commanders and told that the National Intelligence Agency had reported reservations about my suitability to continue as Presidential team leader because of my Security Branch past and in particular an allegation that I had been involved in the Khotso House bombing. I assured my commanders that I had no involvement in that bombing, but they said that they had to discuss the matter with Madiba. I understood, because I certainly would have done the same were I in their shoes. The only condition I agreed with them was that if the president wanted me to be removed, I would have an opportunity to speak to him before leaving my post.

Consequently, they agreed that I could go to the meeting, but would wait outside his office. I think the meeting took all of five minutes and then the door opened. I stood up and Madiba came out, saw me and said: "Yes, Rory, did you enjoy London?" I knew right then that all was okay and that I could continue to serve him.

A few months later when he referred to me in parliament during a debate about affirmative action, it occurred to me that during the meeting with my commanders he did not know (as we had not

129

spoken about it yet) that I wasn't involved in the bombing, yet he was still willing to allow me to continue as his protection team leader! I was astounded and it was then that my loyalty to him was cemented to the extent that I knew beyond any shadow of a doubt that I was prepared to protect him with my life.

After all, who was I but a dispensable white cop who could have been replaced at the drop of a hat?

Years later, after those responsible for bombing Khotso House had either confessed and received amnesty or were convicted and imprisoned, he told me what had transpired behind those closed doors. He said that my commanders wanted me gone, but that he had resisted that notion and insisted that I remain. He said he had told them that it wasn't the foot soldiers that needed to pay for apartheid crimes, but those giving the orders. He felt that I had proved myself to him in the months that I had served him thus far and proved that I had changed my thinking. For him that was precisely what he was trying to achieve in building a nation.

There are so many wonderful memories, which have profoundly influenced me. Many of the life lessons that I was privileged to learn from Madiba up close and personal, I have endeavoured both to implement in my daily life and to teach to my sons. To mention only one example: I will always remember how Madiba went to greet the lady cleaning the floors in the Union Buildings when we arrived early one morning. Everyone mattered equally to him.

I still smile when I remember how we had to adapt our protection strategy to cater for his love of children — if you came out of a building and there were children about, he would always go and talk to them, so we learnt to anticipate that. I would in advance send team members to deploy where the children were and prepare them by asking them not to push and shove but patiently wait for Madiba to greet each one; and of course he always did.

Tata, many, many thanks for the opportunity to serve you and to learn from you, you will forever remain the compass that guides us.

# SONJA
# LOTTER

It was the year 1991. The time when the Winnie Mandela trial was the lead story in the press. I had just started my pupillage at the Johannesburg Bar. One morning as I was on my way to my pupil master's chambers, I entered one of the elevators on ground level in Innes Chambers as usual. The lift was filled with counsel, members from the side bar and a few unfamiliar faces, probably clients on their way to consult with counsel. When I turned around to face the front of the elevator, there he was. Nelson Mandela himself. He was dressed in a grey suit, collar and tie. His physical stature was so impressive it felt like he filled the opening to the lift all by himself, although he had company. With his famous big smile he held out his hand and commenced to greet everyone personally. I was second in line and that moment when his warm smile fell upon me alone and when I was the recipient of his firm handshake is one of the most special moments of my life. But it is not the reason why I shared it with so many people since. It is what happened next, that makes this story so remarkable. After Madiba greeted me he turned to the man who stood next to me and held out his hand to greet the man. The man refused to take Madiba's hand and shook his head. Can you believe it! And so did the man standing next to this man. I was flabbergasted and still am to this day. Madiba did not react in any way and just smiled at them and moved on to the last two people in the lift. But his presence was overwhelming and I knew I was standing in the presence of greatness. A few years later Madiba became our first democratically elected President and he wore Madiba shirts instead of suits.

# WILMÉ
# VERWOERD

I was 4 years old when I first met Madiba. Like most people in their twenties, I don't have many moments from over 18 years ago that I can remember vividly. This is one of those rare exceptions. My younger years took shape during a turbulent political period in South Africa. The country was beginning a journey, transitioning from an oppressive Apartheid regime to a newly formed democracy. Of course I was too young to grasp this at the time. But unlike most white Afrikaans children at the time, I had a mother and a father who had joined the ANC. To give you an idea how unusual this was, it can be summed up pretty quickly. This decision led to my father being ostracized by his family for more than 10 years. A relationship, which still today, bears the scars of this decision. His grandfather was the South African prime minister in the early 1960s perhaps better known as the architect of Apartheid. My mother, the youngest woman MP at the time, was put on death lists by conservative Afrikaans extremists. To an extent, I had some awareness that things were a little different in my house. I met Mandela in parliament in 1996, the day the new Constitution was adopted. My mum had picked me up from the pre-school next door. When we walked through the lobby in parliament, he saw my mum and waved us over. He picked me up in his arms, introduced and asked my name. When he couldn't get the pronunciation right, naturally, I had to correct him. "It's Wilmé not Wilma," I said firmly. He then apologised and said: "I am Nelson Mandela." I found it slightly insulting and to my mum's embarrassment, told him that I knew who he was since I watched television!

Fast forward to 2003. I was now living in Ireland. All traces of my early South African upbringing hidden by my strong Irish accent and pale complexion. Nelson Mandela was to visit Ireland that year to be conferred with an Honorary Doctorate of Law at the University of Galway. He was staying at the Four Seasons in Dublin so like most other people in town that day, I went to the hotel to try and catch a glimpse of him. Walking inside with my father, I was asked to meet my mother (who was the Ambassador) upstairs. She was conversing with Madiba's PA, who told me: "Go into that room over there and wait inside." Who was I to argue, so in I went. Entering the empty room, I sat down on a chair, my dad following closely behind, neither of us really sure of what exactly was going on. I heard a toilet flush. Weird, I thought. Slowly from around the corner I caught a glimpse of someone. In comes walking Nelson Mandela himself. I remember looking around thinking "What the hell?" What followed was something that I will carry with me forever. For more than 20 minutes I sat with my dad and Nelson Mandela. We sat and talked. And now I was old enough to understand what it meant. For Mandela to sit with the grandson of the man who imprisoned him, while at the same time asking me whether I had a boyfriend, was one of the most surreal and significant moments of my life.

# XANDRA
# DE FORTIER

It was a surprise to me when I was told to accompany my executive director to an ANC banquet in the hall of the Greek Orthodox Church. It was one of the first ANC events after the release of Mr Mandela and possibly even the first in Pretoria.

I was excited but slightly apprehensive as to whether Mr Mandela would be present. After all, my husband had been involved with his transfer from Robben Island to Pollsmoor. I knew that Madiba would realise who I was if I should be introduced to him, and shared my apprehension with my executive director. It was very soon after his release, the negotiations at Kempton Park were balanced on a knife-edge, and one could not help wondering how Mr Mandela would react when he realised my connection.

On arrival we studied the table placings. If I remember correctly we were seated at table 19, the table in the middle of the hall. Sharing the table with us would be an ambassador, an official of the Hellenic community, a past editor of the *Rand Daily Mail*, and someone representing the Chamber of Commerce – as well as an empty seat with no name indicated.

Organizing functions, with the accompanying protocol of table placements, was part of my duties and something with which I was well acquainted. I realised immediately that this had to be the main table. And the empty seat? At the back of my mind I knew already who would be sitting there, but I did not share my suspicion with my executive director, because ignorance is sometimes bliss.

We were told to take our places. We stepped forward, exchanged greetings and introductions and everybody sat down. Except the occupant of the empty chair. A choir treated us to a few songs, until suddenly silence fell – I would almost say a sacred silence. There he stood in the main entrance – Mr. Nelson Mandela.

His unmistakable presence filled the room as he moved easily from table to table, greeting everyone and chatting amicably – first all the tables at the sides, then those in the inner circle, finally reaching table 19. He moved around the table, being introduced to everybody he did not know. I was also introduced and ex-plained that I was accompanying the executive director for the evening. As I expected, he deduced from my surname who I was. "Are you his wife?" he asked. I confirmed this and mentioned that he had died. He took both my hands in his, looked me in the eyes and replied:" I am sorry. I am really sorry to hear that. Do you know that your husband was a remarkably good man?" My mind was in turmoil. I had not expected this.

Of course he mentioned some details about his boat trip to Cape Town, his stay in prison and the conversations he had while he was there. We listened with bated breaths. The evening passed all too soon. Mr Mandela said goodbye to everybody at our table and again went from table to table shaking hands with the other guests. He started walking towards the entrance, but turned around suddenly and came back to our table. He again took my hands in his and said: "Remember, he was a good man".

His last words to me were typical of the man and how we would come to know Nelson Mandela: "Are you well taken care of? And how are the boys, three of them if I can remember correctly?"

To say that the evening was deeply emotional is truly to reduce the whole experience. I will hopefully remember for the rest of my life his last words to me that evening and tell it to as many people as I can.

Do I have regrets? Yes, but regret always comes too late. I regret that I did not use the opportunity to thank Mr Mandela for the friendly words to me that evening. I was just too scared that it would look arrogant or pretentious. However, it always means so much to hear kind words about the love of your life, whose loss you will forever mourn.

So let me say now: "Dankie Tata en rus sag." (Thank you Tata. Rest peacefully.)

# GRATITUDE

"It was only when I was
in jail that I wondered,
'What happened to
so-and-so? Why didn't I
go back and say
thank you?'"

NELSON MANDELA

# CLIVE NOBLE

Before my retirement, I was an orthopedic surgeon in Johannesburg. During the apartheid era I was asked to treat Winnie Madikizela Mandela who was under house arrest in Brandfort at the time.

Following successful surgery she returned to Brandfort. I subsequently had to also treat their daughter Zinzi. Winnie was required to return to see me for reassessment periodically. She was, and is, a very interesting woman. Knowing that I was a member of the Boxing Board of Control at the time, she always asked me about my assessment of boxers in upcoming fights. One day I asked her why she was so interested in boxing. She answered that she was not at all interested in boxing. I wanted to know why she asked me all these questions about boxing and she said: "Nelson wants to know." Madiba was still in prison.

In 1992, I was the South African team doctor at the Barcelona Olympics. Nelson Mandela arrived at the Olympic village and we were all asked to stand in line to meet him. There were about 120 people in the team. When he got to me we shook hands and I introduced myself as Clive Noble. I did not say I was a doctor. He held my hand for a long time, looked at me and said: "I want to thank you for helping my family in very difficult times." I was totally amazed that he remembered my name and who I was.

I met him subsequently at sporting events including the 1995 Rugby World Cup where I was the match doctor. A while after the initial meeting, he arrived one Sunday evening at a gymnasium near his house in Johannesburg. I was a member at the gym and was exercising at the time. I showed him around the gymnasium and at the end of the short tour he asked me how much I thought they would charge him to train there. He was about 70 years old at the time.

Of course I said that I did not think they would charge him. Always humble, always friendly. He was indeed a great man.

# FARIEDA OMAR

I used to have a fruit and vegetable stall at the Salt River market. During all the years Mandela was on Robben Island, I sent a bag of fruit every time a lawyer visited him on Robben Island. Only once did the guards let that through. Mandela sent a personal thank you. He said it was the first time in 19 years that he'd seen a banana.

# FUMBATILE MBILINI

In 1996 Hlumelo Biko (son of Steve Biko) was going through his traditional initiation in Ginsberg, Eastern Cape. We had just taken Hlumelo to initiation school when we saw police and a helicopter hovering above Ginsberg. At around 1 pm in the afternoon Madiba arrived, had a short meeting with Biko's wife, Ntsiki, and then came to meet those of us who had gathered at the small kraal behind Biko's house. We sat with Madiba, together with Hlumelo's traditional nurse, Tshingana Mbena, for nearly two hours.

At about 3pm Mandela asked to be taken to Hlumelo's circumcision school, but by then it had started raining. Without hesitation I gave him my jacket so he could cover himself. In our culture we know that when we speak to an initiate, especially when giving advice, a man needs to wear a jacket. So the jacket served two purposes, rain and custom.

I had bought the jacket at a second-hand shop in East London two weeks before Mandela's visit. I knew about the visit and was very nervous about meeting a man of Madiba's stature. But when he arrived and started talking, I started gaining confidence and realised that Madiba was human and humble.

When I gave Tata the jacket, I did not expect anything in return. He told his bodyguards to take my details and that was the end of it . . . It shocked me when I received an SMS message a week later that I should go and collect a voucher for a R1000. I bought myself some shirts and got the rest in cash.

# NAVIN
# MORAT

I met Madiba at an official function held at State House in his honour during his first visit to Namibia soon after his release.

I was introduced to him as the first person of Indian origin to have settled in the then South West Africa (in 1977). (There was a law that precluded us from settling there, much like it was in the Orange Free State.)

He enquired of me if I knew of another Indian lady who had married a German orthopedic surgeon and had settled in Windhoek. Her name was Deborah Opitz. When I confirmed that I did indeed know her, he immediately expressed the desire to meet her whereupon I offered to arrange the meeting.

When I left the function I excitedly contacted Deborah and related what had transpired and the meeting was arranged.

Debbie, as she is fondly known, was a nurse and one of the few persons who were charged with nursing Madiba while he was in prison and secretly brought to Cape Town when he needed medical attention.

What I find most amazing, as do most people I relate the incident to, is that this great figure, with all the hype surrounding him at the time, actually remembered her and followed her whereabouts. The greatness of this personality is truly mind-bogglingly amazing.

# NOKUZOLA MABHIJA

Post 1994, I was a member of staff in Parliament. I remember the day I was walking with a friend along one of the ground floor passages in Parliament connecting the New Wing and the Old Assembly.

In the middle of the passage we met Mr Mandela and his body-guards. We were so excited meeting him for the first time that we were unable to move back against the wall to let him pass. His bodyguards ordered us to do so and we eventually submitted to the order. But Mr Mandela disregarded his bodyguards and instead came over to us, as we were standing against the wall. He shook our hands and initiated a small conversation with us.

In the conversation he thanked us for supporting Members of Parliament. I was excited by that encounter with Mr. Nelson Mandela. It impacted on my patriotism and boosted my work spirit.

# RICHARD LAPCHICK

I was incredibly blessed to be invited to the inauguration of Nelson Mandela because of my work in leading the American sports boycott of South Africa from the mid 1970s until the end of apartheid. After the inauguration I was with President Mandela in his box at the Zambia vs. South Africa soccer match in Johannesburg. He chose to go there instead of all the diplomatic parties in Pretoria where the inauguration was held.

I asked him why he went to the game instead of to the receptions in his honour. He responded: "I wanted my people to know that I appreciate the sacrifices our athletes made during all the years of the sports boycott. If it were not for them I would not have become president so soon."

It was the ultimate power-of-sport story for me. We were in the same stadium where the Rugby World Cup would be held one year later. I have no doubt that President Mandela was thinking about how he would use that event to help bring his people together and heal the racial divide in South Africa.

# SALLY
# ROWNEY

I received the following message written on an
ANC message pad:

*Dear Sally*

*A thousand thanks for everything you have done for us. Compliments and best wishes.*

*Sincerely Madiba*

The phone rang at about four in the afternoon on February 12, 1990. It was my friend Jean de la Harpe. She worked for the National Reception Committee for the release of the leaders. "Sally, can you and your five children vacate your house tonight? We need to accommodate a family of seven near Lanseria airport. Keep your phone line open so I can get through to you." I knew immediately who one of those family members was. I had one condition – that I could meet him. Jean agreed immediately and in the next breath asked if I wouldn't mind cooking dinner for "him" and the other family members. She wasn't sure how many other people to expect, but did warn me that there were a "few small planes" expected to arrive at Lanseria. Madiba was coming for dinner and possibly staying the night!

We had little time to change all the sheets and no time to shop, so I had to look deep into the freezer and take out food, organise alternative accommodation for myself and the children and think about cooking. My housekeeper, Elizabeth Mathebula, organised a friend to help us cook. About two hours later, before the gate intercom rang, we heard the helicopters circling closer and closer overhead. As the car pulled into the garage, there was a bolt of lightning and the electricity went out. A typical Johannesburg storm was brewing.

Madiba had to enter the house from the garage into a darkish kitchen. My children, who had been excitedly watching the helicopters outside, had rushed inside due to the big drops of rain. He was welcomed in the kitchen by a line of five little kids. My excited six-year-old son exclaimed: "Are you Mr Mandela? I saw you on television yesterday!" With a wide grin on his face, Madiba bent down and gave him a hug, followed by hugs for my other children, who all huddled around him with outstretched arms. He greeted us all so warmly.

That day we welcomed more than seven people. Immediately behind him, the kitchen was soon crowded with the rest of the entourage: his wife Winnie, his daughters, grandchildren, Frank Chikane, Cyril Ramaphosa, Eric Molobi, Jay Naidoo, Saki Macozoma, Murphy Morobe, Valli Moosa and so many other leaders I cannot recall — for I was filling pots with food, apart from making arrangements to light the house with candles and pulling out gas cookers.

Cars continued to arrive and every chair in the house was moved to the living room. Even then some people were sitting on cushions on the floor. Drinks were served. Walter and Albertina Sisulu arrived and sat together on the sofa chatting to Madiba — an unforgettable reunion.

The garden also started to fill up with young ANC "lions", who were deployed to act as security. That is when packets of food were delivered to the back door. The electricity came back on. I had no idea how many people were inside the house or outside, but I do know that, even with all the packets of food that covered the kitchen counter and with the freezer empty, there still was not enough. We cooked and cooked. Supper was served. Everyone ate on their laps. Plates moved back and forth from the kitchen to the living room and from the kitchen to the garden. I can't remember how many plates of food were served that night. But it did not matter, we could have cooked all night. This was our moment in history – the night Madiba came to dinner.

Everyone watched the eight o'clock news, the children sitting at Madiba's feet watching with him. "Where had Mr Mandela been taken on his second night out of Victor Verster? A house in North Riding or Honeydew?" "Crowds have surrounded the Soweto home of Mr Mandela expecting him any moment . . ." I remember thinking how strange it was to see history in the making while it was happening in my own home. One of the children pointed to the television, turned to Madiba and said: "Look, there you are!" And then the planning began for the next day. Madiba was busy preparing his speech for the rally at FNB Stadium, how he was going to get there and many more details. And so, into the evening, the discussions went on.

Much later he was shown to the bedrooms and left to go to bed, guarded by the ANC "lions" outside. We were privileged to have shared such a moment in history with him.

And so I want to say:

*Dear Madiba*

*A thousand thanks for everything YOU have done for us South Africans. You are and always will be our hero.*

# HUMILITY

"I stand here before you
not as a prophet,
but as a humble
servant of you,
the people."

NELSON MANDELA

# ALBERT NTUNJA

I remember on a certain Saturday morning when Mr Mandela was President, he came to the parliamentary library where I still work. I was alone in the library on that day and the library was closed – the parliament library closes on a Saturday. I was surprised to see the President. He asked me for information on the Premiers of the nine South African provinces. My response was that the library was closed but I promised him to try my level best to assist him. When I said the library was closed he accepted that and told me not to worry about the information he wanted. I could not believe that the President came to the library himself to look for information instead of asking an aid to do so in the first place, especially given his extraordinary status in the country.

# ANGELIQUE KIDJO

The first meeting with Madiba was a very spiritual and uplifting one for me and had a deep impact on my life. On 29 November 2003, the day before the first 46664 Concert in Cape Town, all the artists were invited to join Madiba on Robben Island. In the middle of the visit and with everyone there, Beyonce, Annie Lennox, the guys from Queen etcetera, I unexpectedly ended up very close to Madiba. He looked at me and said: "I know that you are an artist, but where are you from?"

I answered him and then I said: "Thank you very much for all you have done and all the sacrifices you have been through". And he responded: "Don't thank me. We all have our fights to fight. That is what I was supposed to do and what you are doing is part of the fight too."

And within that crowded place with everyone there he made me feel so special, by engaging with me directly. What he said to me that day, i.e. that we are all capable of moving mountains really resonated in me and changed my life. Since then, every time I struggle with something and I doubt that I can manage or cope, the memory of him and how he truly believed that we are all special and have the power to change things in the world, brings me right back on track and gives me the strength to carry on.

I met Madiba again a few years later in June 2005 in Tromso, Norway at another 46664 concert. And it was amazing. He actually remembered me and said: "Hey, my girl, you are here. Now I know the event is going to go well." And I was so taken aback. I mean the fact that he remembered me and then said these beautiful things. I am not that special. Of all the amazing artists that were there he remembered me and as with the time on Robben Island he made me feel so special.

What was so extraordinary about Madiba is that he always made himself available to people no matter how difficult it might be under the circumstances and when he spoke to you he engaged with you as if you were the only one there and made you feel as if you are a very special person.

He was so powerful and yet he stayed so humble.

# DESMOND TUTU

During a hearing of the Amnesty Committee at the Truth and Reconciliation Commission, one of the applicants, Bennet Sibaya, suggested that one of the Commissioners Dumisa Ntsebeza's car was used as a getaway car in the brutal Helderberg Tavern massacre. To make matters worse he then identified Ntsebeza as the driver of the car.

Naturally that threw the TRC in crisis. I immediately went to Madiba to ask for an independent judicial commission to be appointed to investigate the matter so that the credibility of the TRC would not be undermined. Madiba appointed former Constitutional Court judge, Richard Goldstone to investigate the matter. Some time later, I got a call early on a Sunday morning from Madiba's assistant at Groote Schuur who wanted to know if I had a personal contact for Dumisa Ntsebeza. I knew immediately that it was typical of Madiba. I knew that he must have seen the report from Justice Goldstone, which as it turned out would confirm that the allegations were false and that he (Madiba) wanted to put Dumisa at ease about the findings.

But I felt strongly that this was not the correct procedure and asked Madiba's assistant to convey the message. I said: "Please tell the President that I am the chair of the Truth Commission and I must be the first to see the report. Also if there is something to be communicated with one of the commissioners it should be me." She promised to do so.

I had barely put the phone down, when it rang again. This time it was Madiba himself on the other side. "Mpilo," he said, using my African name. "Mpilo, I wanted to say you are right and I am sorry. I apologise for not speaking to you first."

How extraordinary! Very few people apologise when they do something wrong, but even far fewer presidents will acknowledge a mistake and then go as far as personally apologise – and so quickly and generously. To me it shows the incredible humility of this great man.

# KARINA TUROK

We were at the Constantia home of the Menel family, when Mandela was chatting with a fellow prisoner from the Island, in the lounge. Eddie Daniel's seven-year-old grandson arrived to meet with Madiba for the first time. Madiba stood up from the comfort of a low couch to shake hands with the young boy, and said to him: "I am so honoured to meet with you." His respect for other people, no matter their age or background was something I had never witnessed from anyone ever before.

# MORNÉ DU PLESSIS

I was privileged to be a close bystander and participant, as manager of the Springbok team in 1995, (that won the Rugby World Cup), in the epic events that unfolded when the great statesman, Nelson Mandela, united a nation by supporting a rugby team. This great sporting story has been documented in many ways, not least in the film *Invictus*, starring Morgan Freeman and Matt Damon. This film while understandably not able to sketch all the details, does closely describe the events of the day and the great political risk taken by President Mandela to wear a Springbok rugby shirt and support a team that would to many have been the symbol of oppression and prejudice that had been part of the South African landscape. My own explanation of this act of true statemanship, is that his intentions were personal and sincere (rather than politically calculated), as a signal of reconciliation .

It was during this unforgettable time of the World Cup of 1995 that I was privileged to meet President Mandela on a few occasions.

In the year 2000, the South African Press club held a dinner to honour the "Newsmakers of the Year" for the last decade and present an award to the "Newsmaker of the Decade". Obviously this award would be presented to Madiba, and the 1995 World Cup Rugby Team, as one of the winners during that 10 year period, was invited to the event. I was asked to represent the team at this function which I did with honour.

President Mandela attended the function, received his award, addressed the 500 strong audience and understandably because of his age and busy schedule, retired early from the function. As he made his way out of the function room to a standing and adoring ovation, he passed near the table at the back of the function room where I was standing. I must have caught his eye (possibly because I am nearly 2 metres tall), and he suddenly and to my absolute surprise changed course and walked directly towards me with a big smile. Much in the vein of not addressing the King or Queen until you have been addressed, I waited for his first response, which came in the words that left me even more speechless.

"Ah Morné, (and after a pause) — do you still remember me?"

I carry this moment with me as an important event in my life. These few words, in this circumstance, illustrate a great humility and "humanness" of this great man and his ability to make those around him feel important, whoever they were.

It certainly made me feel good and does even now as I write this.

# REBECCA HAYES

It was 1996 and I was 18 years old getting ready for my Matric final exam. I had been complaining of major earache and throat pain, so my mom made an appointment for me to see our ENT specialist, Dr. Brian Wolfowitz, in Rosebank.

My dad took me and when we arrived we noticed a black limo parked outside the rooms. I was in so much pain that we didn't even think twice about whom it was for and just headed straight to reception.

Once we checked in with the receptionist we waited and waited and waited. My dad was getting quite worried as my ear and throat pain was getting worse and it was an hour past my appointment. He went to the receptionist and politely asked what the hold up was. She whispered to my dad: "The President has an emergency appointment: "Needless to say my dad turned around, sat down and waited patiently.

Not long after that, some bodyguards walked through followed by Nelson Mandela. The entire waiting room was in complete shock and all my pain completely disappeared. Mr Mandela spoke quietly to his bodyguard, who then spoke quietly to the receptionist. She then pointed at me!

The President of South Africa at that time, a Nobel Peace prize-winner and one of the most famous men in the world, walked over to me and apologised for taking my appointment! I was totally stunned and didn't quite know what to say except: "It's cool".

He shook my hand and asked my name, how old I was and what I wanted to do after I matriculated. Being a typical teenager and without any consideration of the fact that I was speaking to the President of South Africa and his feelings, I said that I would like to move to America. Of all the things to say! Mr Mandela gave a little chuckle and graciously said: "That's good. Then you can bring your American boyfriend that you will meet back to South Africa".

Before I knew it the bodyguards were at his side. He said goodbye and good luck to me and walked out the door and got into the black limo. I only noticed at that point the South African flags on the corners of the bonnet.

As I stood there forgetting about all the pain in my ears and throat and listening to the chatter of excitement amongst the other patients and staff, all I could think was: *He's much taller than I thought*. But most of all I remembered his eyes which were slightly milky in colour, but so gentle, kind and honest. What a man!

Just to end off my story that I will never forget for the rest of my life . . . it turned out I had mumps!

I am now thirty-five years old, still living in Joburg, married (to a true South African man) and have two wonderful boys who love it when I tell them about my fifteen minutes of fame!

# SERGIO DOS SANTOS

Shortly after Madiba was released, I was coaching the Cape Town Spurs soccer team. We had just played a match in Durban on a Sunday afternoon and were at Durban airport to catch our return flight to Cape Town.

Suddenly there was a lot of activity and reactions from people looking in a certain direction. Soon it became obvious why. The one and only Nelson Mandela walked into one of the departure halls with an entourage of people. Upon seeing him, I nearly collapsed. I was so excited. So I started to clap, then my players started to clap and then everyone around the airport started to clap.

He had noticed that it was me who started the applause and he walked straight over to me. He said: "Good afternoon! And who might you be?" I said: "Well, I am Sergio do Santos, manager and coach of Cape Town Spurs." And he said: "I am Nelson." It was just unbelievable to me. Not only was he speaking to me, but he introduced himself as if I did not know who he was! So humble.

So after he shook my hand he asked against whom we had played that afternoon. So I told him and then he said: "Would you please introduce me to your boys?" So of course I introduced him to the team and he greeted everyone individually and shook hands. He then proceeded to tell me that he was aware that we were at that stage attempting to be promoted into the Premier League of soccer in South Africa and that he wished us the very best. He said that he was a soccer fan and followed the matches.

To have been in the presence of that man would be with me for the rest of my life. It was so emotional; it was a feeling that I think you will only otherwise get at the birth of your first child. It is a feeling that you cannot put into words and will be with you for the rest of your life.

To me it was just unbelievable that his tall, gigantic man, came down to our level, shook our hands and wishing us the best. It was a dream come true and an experience that can only be described as: *being in the presence of light*.

# SHIRLEY NAIDOO

As his housekeeper, I got to know Madiba as the most humble and considerate man. One day after breakfast he had his normal small cup of coffee in the lounge. He put his feet on the foot rest and having just polished his shoes a small bit of black polish rubbed off on the cream fabric of the foot rest. I got a call from a very apologetic Madiba who said: "Darling, I am so sorry, but I messed up your couch. My sincere apologies." As if any of us minded. That's Madiba for you.

He also frequently did a lot for himself. I remember on one occasion in 2001, when one of the cleaners forgot to put down the bathroom mats for him for the morning. I only realised it late at night and felt so bad, but did not want to disturb Madiba. When I apologized to him the next morning he was totally puzzled and said: "No, no! What are you talking about? Don't be silly, I did it myself." And the bathroom mats were laid out, perfectly straight, on the floor of his bathroom.

This came as no surprise to me, since he was always meticu-lously neat. I am not sure if it was just his personality or from his time in jail. For example, when he finished reading the newspaper, he would painstakingly straighten and fold it perfectly, so that it was impossible to know that he had read it. It looked totally unopened. And when he folded his shirts, it was always perfectly done.

# SUMAYAH FORTUNE

I am the communications projects office manager in Parliament. The most memorable encounter I had with Madiba was during the State of the Nation Address one year. The encounter happened after the ceremony and activities of the day had taken place. The theme for the year was about disability. We took the disabled guests after the occasion to Tuynhuys to meet Madiba.

When we arrived there as staff members of Parliament, we all stood together to one side trying to be out of the way, waiting for our guests to speak to Madiba. We were going to take them back to Parliament afterwards.

Madiba was enjoying himself and after speaking to the guests, he came over to us staff members and asked us whether we would mind terribly if he could take a picture with us. I think almost all of us were shocked and surprised. It took us a moment to respond. We never forgot it.

# INCLUSIVITY

"If you talk to a man
in a language he
understands, that goes to
his head. If you talk
to him in his language,
that goes to his heart."

NELSON MANDELA

# AMANDA BOTHA

It was a short meeting – in May 1992 – in the presence of Adéle Searle, as hostess. Her Club 100 was receiving Nelson Mandela in a Cape hotel as speaker that day. I was there early with my copy of "I am Prepared to Die", Mandela's book which was published in 1979 by the International Defense Aid Fund. I bought it in London, when it was banned in South Africa, and had more or less kept it hidden until that day. If the occasion presented itself, I wanted to ask him to sign it for me.

Unexpectedly Adéle called me and introduced me to him. He held my hand in his for a moment, and with a surname like Botha he knew immediately that I spoke Afrikaans. "Aangename kennis, bly om te ontmoet" ("I'm pleased to meet you") he said. Nervously I asked for his signature, which he readily gave, and when I thanked him, he held me back for a moment to say that he was an admirer of Afrikaans literature.

I had to control myself to make sure that I had heard him correctly, especially when he continued: "I liked reading Afrikaans books on Robben Island. I had the *Groot Verseboek* (an iconic collection of Afrikaans poetry) and often read from it. I read *Bart Nel* (about a man who rebels against the existing order and loses everything). I also read some of F.A.Venter's books, but Langenhoven was a favourite," he said while smiling warmly.

I was dumbstruck. There were still a few seconds left before someone else would claim him. The man whom I had let myself picture so differently, continued: "I am looking forward to reading more Afrikaans. I didn't have a wide choice. I ordered *Groot Verseboek* myself." Before he was introduced to someone else, he said: "I am glad to have met you."

I had my signed copy in my hand. I was overwhelmed by the short meeting – the sincerity, the friendliness and enthusiasm. Afterwards I couldn't really concentrate. I wrote down the Afrikaans word *meelewend*. There is not an exact English translation. Directly translated it means: *to live with or together*.

*Meelewend* with **me**. I am Afrikaans and the literature touches a deep-lying artery in me. The moment is too staggering for any scepticism. I excitedly tell others about the meeting, but nobody seems to believe me.

And then it came like a flood. Mandela's famous opening of the first democratically elected Parliament in May 1994 when he read out – admittedly in English – Ingrid Jonker's poem *The child*. Shortly afterwards Tafelberg Publishers announced that Mandela, while still a prisoner on Robben Island, had written them a letter to thank them for sending *Groot Verseboek* which he had ordered.

In the next year or two there appeared many reports mentioning Mandela's interest in and appreciation for Afrikaans literature.

Writers like Elsa Joubert and Klaas Steytler were invited to dinner at his Cape residence, Genadendal, and they talk enthusiastically about the meeting. Karel Schoeman was honoured by him for his contribution to Afrikaans literature. And would you believe, Madiba himself (with Zelda la Grange by his side goes off to the bookshop to buy J.C. Kannemeyer's biography of C.J. Langenhoven.

My moment with the man who had the world at his feet and who, amongst all the bustle, took a few minutes to tell me that he appreciated the language of my heart, and read and appreciated the books we write in this language, filled me with hope. Later, he even told the world that he cherished the language. The language with its own struggle history which once was despised and which was the match that set alight the Soweto riots of 1976 – **thìs** language and its writers were appreciated and enjoyed as literature by **him**. Even more, the language became part of his arsenal with which to effect reconciliation across boundaries. **That** was my moment of inner transformation in our country, which we all love for so many different reasons. Madiba, who I now accepted without inner denial, became my champion. His disposition would wipe out boundaries and build bridges, I realized at that moment.

# AUDREY CHANDLER

My late husband, Robin Chandler was the owner of Chandler Appointments in Cape Town. Robin's close friend Morakile Shuenyani (who worked for Engen at the time and was the founder of Black Enterprise Magazine amongst many other distinctions) arranged for Robin to accompany him to the Mandela home for a cocktail party during 1990 or thereabouts. The pair arrived at the Mandela home, and Robin was duly briefly introduced to Madiba by name. After chatting for some time with various guests, Chris Hani being one of them (who jokingly gave Robin the honorary title of General within the ANC party as a white man amongst what I gathered were mainly black guests) Madiba beckoned to Robin to come and sit beside him on the sofa to chat. Robin was astounded that with the very many guests, Madiba had not only remembered and addressed him by his name, but also remembered where Robin came from and all just on the introduction alone. They chatted for some time whilst one of Madiba's grandchildren sat on his knee.

For Robin, this was a remarkable and humbling experience that Madiba treated this white stranger as a friend and as important a guest as anybody else.

# FRANCOIS PIENAAR

Shortly after the World Cup I was at the Union Buildings for a function with my then fiancée Nerine. I had only once before mentioned her name to Madiba, but he came over to us and surprised both of us by calling Nerine by her name and asked how we both were. He then took Nerine aside and asked if she would be offended if he were to come to our wedding.

We were stunned and of course the answer was: "Please come!"

And those were not just empty words, he actually came. Madiba and his daughter, Zindzi attended and insisted to sit amongst every one. No fuss, no protocol, no special requirements. As if it was totally normal for not only the President of the country, but Nelson Mandela, to attend our wedding!

A few years later in 1998, our son Jean was born while we were living in London. Four days after his birth, the phone rang early in the morning on Nerine's side of the bed. Nerine picked up and a long conversation followed clearly with the other person inquiring about her health and how our little baby was doing. I kept on encouraging her to put the phone down, not for a moment believing that it could be Madiba, until he asked to talk to me. He congratulated me on my son's birth and then asked if we would possibly consider bestowing the honour on him of being Jean's godfather! Of course the honour was all ours. Madiba then said that my son's Xhosa name would be: *Mkhokeli* (leader).

In 1999 our second son Stephane was born. About 6 years later Nerine, myself and the two boys went for tea at Madiba's Houghton house. Over the years I had been asked many times to have tea with Madiba and from time to time the family went along. However, on the way to Houghton in the car that day Stephane was clearly deep in thought, contemplating something. As soon as we arrived and he saw Madiba, he stormed over to him and asked: "Madiba, will you please be my godfather too." Madiba laughed, put his arm around him and said: "I would be honoured. I can see that you are a courageous and brave one. I will name you *Ghora* (the brave one).

# LAURIE WEBBER

In 1993, I happened to go down to Umhlanga Beach to take my young daughter to play. As she was only a year old at the time I carried her on my shoulders. On arrival at the beach I saw a large crowd of people standing on the sidewalk and asked them what was happening. Someone said that Nelson Mandela was on the beach. I asked where exactly he was as there were only a few people standing talking on the actual beach. Someone pointed out where he was, and, as I could not subdue my curiousty or the desire to meet him, I went down onto the sand and walked to where Mr Mandela was.

Without much ado I introduced myself to him. He shook my hand and chatted for a few minutes with me. In the brief moment that I was with him he greeted my daughter as well clearly showing his deep love for "little people". The sincere manner in which he spoke to her made me realize what a positive attitude he had towards all people.

I was also very impressed at the humble and friendly manner in which he communicated with total strangers. This left me with a lasting impression that if anyone could, this man would be capable of making our country a safe and happy place for all races to live in.

Having spent only a few minutes with Nelson Madela I was fortunate to experience his amazing personality and felt sure that he would be a great asset as a future leader and President of South Africa. I also believed that he would be instrumental in making our country a truly *Rainbow Nation*.

# MARLEEN POTGIETER

A friend of mine, Inga van Huysteen, phoned me during November 2000 and said, "Hi Marleen, even if you are doing something on the 5th February 2001 you are not doing anything. Clear your diary and the date is cast in stone. We are going to have dinner with President Mandela." I was shocked. "What – ?" I asked. "Have coffee with me and I will tell you the story," she replied. We met at Cafe Paradiso, which was owned by a mutual friend and she told me the story.

A long-time friend of Inga's from their early politicking and activism days, Robin Carlisle, invited her to a DP function, where President Mandela was going to address some of the senior members of the DP at a dinner organised by Tony Leon. During his speech Mandela said two things, which infuriated my easily riled friend. She has a heightened sense of justice and will challenge anyone who transgresses her line of what should or should not be done. He said that the ANC should be forgiven for some political foibles as they were a young ruling party and had a lot to learn. He also said that white people were leaving the country in droves and were not committed to this country. It is the latter statement, which particularly raised her hackles. Penning a hasty note on a serviette, she handed it to the then presidential spokesperson, Parks Makhahlana, asking him to give it to the President at the first available opportunity. Looking at the note, President Mandela looked up into the audience and said, "Mrs Van Huysteen, I believe you have something to say." She addressed the President regarding his comment on the purported lack of parliamentary skills of the ruling party, but it was the second comment that prompted the chain-reaction. She said: "I take umbrage at your statement that white people are not committed to this country. I am committed and so are all my friends. In fact, I don't know anybody in my circle of friends who is not committed and your statement is just wrong," at which she sat down.

A few days later she received the phone call that all of us believe will never happen to us: "Is this Mrs van Huysteen?" "Yes it is". "This is President Mandela on the line. Are you and your husband busy on Thursday? I would like you to come for some tea". If she was, she was instantly not busy and she and her husband visited the President in his home at Genadendal, where President Mandela personally served them tea. During this meeting he asked her about her statement on the commitment of white people. She repeated that **all** of her friends were committed South Africans. It was in response to this statement, that the President asked her if she could gather twenty of her friends and invite them all to a dinner at his house. He stipulated certain conditions. We were each to prepare a little talk about who we were, what we did and how we could show our commitment to this country. She said that she certainly could and definitely would . . . hence her phone-call to me.

On the day of the dinner, I had spent the day in Johannesburg on business. On the flight home, I could hardly contain my excitement. Dinner was to be early, as the President did not like late nights. We were to gather in the reception room for drinks, where he would meet us, as was protocol and we would all go together into the diningroom, where we would present our pieces between courses. I had it all planned. I would land, run to the car, get changed into a fresh suit in the car, put on lip-stick and drive straight to the President's house on Edinburgh Drive in Newlands. But, I couldn't find my car. Now quite late, I was frantically running around the car park thinking about the wet underarm patches; there was now no time to change. I eventually paid one of those courtesy golf-cart drivers R200 to drive up and down the car park to find my car. I arrived in the nick of time.

We were gathered in the reception room, sipping sherry, wondering how and when we would see the great man. We were all milling about, chatting, not concentrating on anything anybody was saying, when suddenly he was amongst us. Such was his charisma that it was as though an electric current had passed through the room. I sensed him before I saw him. He really was a larger than life person and his size was increased by his aura.

He had done his homework. He worked the room, smiling, talking in that distinctive voice of his and chatting to everyone. When introduced to everyone around the room, he knew who we were and where we were from. When he got to me, he engulfed my hand in his huge hand. "Mrs Potgieter! You work for Mallinicks. The firm of the Islanders. It is indeed a privilege to meet you!"

(Mallinicks, the law firm, where I was practising as a partner specialising in labour law, is where Tokyo Sexwale's wife Judy had worked as a para-legal and through the work the firm did with several political prisoners incarcerated on Robben Island, we got the reputation of being the law-firm of the Islanders. That he had found out about that, shows the mark of the man – less humble leaders never bother to find out about other, less important people.) I mumbled something to the effect that it was I, who felt privileged. He flashed a smile at me.

Jelly-legged, I followed the group into the dining room. With the tunnel vision that such an occasion brings, I fixated on the gold leafed plates at my setting, adorned with the Presidential crest. The house is beautiful, full of colonial furniture and very presidential. Mandela proceeded to tell us a story. He asked us, if we had noticed the security guard at the gate. I cannot remember his name, but it was a name like Van der Merwe, which I shall call him here. On leaving Genadendal one morning, he noticed that Van der Merwe was not on duty. He asked his aide if he was sick. No, the aide said, he had been asked to leave. President Mandela was taken aback – why, had he done something wrong? No, the aide answered, since he had served President De Klerk, it was assumed that Mandela would not want him there. Mandela immediately reinstated Van der Merwe, who turned out to be his most loyal servant and completely committed to his job.

We presented our prepared talks and after each presentation, President Mandela would comment, addressing the speaker directly. I was so proud to be part of this gathering. At some stage during the evening, he turned to Phumzile Ngcuka, patting her arm in a father-like manner and said: "This young lady is going to go very far". She blushed and looked down meekly. At that stage, none of us knew who she was, but he turned out to be right. She has come far, becoming the woman to hold the highest office ever held by a woman in our country – that of Deputy President.

We had been told that Mandela does not like to stay up late and were asked to leave at 9. At eleven that night, he was still talking. He became conversational and told us stories. The one story that I remember, is that he told us the thing he missed the most, while he was in prison, was the sound of children's voices. He told us that children were very special to him and was the reason why he had started a foundation for children. We felt like very special guests indeed. I will never forget the evening and it is an amazing name-dropping announcement to make at dinner-parties!

# MELANIE VERWOERD

Shortly after the 1994 elections, I received a call from Madiba's private secretary, who explained that President Mandela was hosting representatives of thirty conservative Afrikaner women's organisations for tea the next morning in Pretoria. He wanted me to accompany him the next morning. Of course I was delighted, albeit slightly apprehensive.

Early the next morning I arrived at the military airbase on the outskirts of Cape Town. I was shown to a waiting room and a few minutes later Madiba arrived, flanked by two bodyguards. Madiba knew all the staff by name and took time to greet them and ask after their families. After he gave me a big hug, we started to make our way in the dark to the small presidential jet across the tarmac. Madiba suddenly spotted a man sweeping the grounds in the distance. He insisted that the worker be brought over, so he could greet him. "This always happens," one of the bodyguards next to me said with a groan. "It takes us forever to get anywhere!"

As soon as we were in the air, the bodyguards fell asleep, but Madiba was bright-eyed and wanted to chat. He also wanted to practise his speech for the morning – which was in Afrikaans – on me. He read it a few times, pausing when he needed help with the Afrikaans pronunciation. I told him how touched I was by the effort he was making. "Language is important when it comes to reconciliation," he conceded. "You know, my only problem is that with my hearing being so bad, I struggle to hear Afrikaans. So please stay close to me, to help me if I need translation."

At the official residence, Madiba went to his office for a few minutes and I was shown into the room by Madiba's housekeeper, Jacques Human. "Ladies, can I get your attention please," said Jacques in Afrikaans. "I would like to introduce you to Melanie Verwoerd. She is a member of parliament accompanying President Mandela today. She is of course from"– he paused for dramatic effect – 'the ANC." It felt like hundreds of blue-eye-shadowed eyes had turned to me with cold hatred. "Good luck!" Jacques whispered, and made a hasty escape.

There was a few seconds' silence before the women resumed their conversations, ignoring me. Then one woman, who was clearly the leader of the group, called them all to order. "Ladies," she said sternly, "before Mandela arrives, I want us to agree on a few house rules. We have to remember that we are here to make a point, to send a message. So can we remind ourselves that we will only speak Afrikaans today. Even if we are asked to speak English, or Mandela speaks English, we will stick to Afrikaans." There were loud cheers of support, and the leader triumphantly pulled her jacket into place.

Thinking of Mandela practising his speech on the early-morning flight, I felt an anger rising in me. However, before I could say anything, I spotted Madiba through the window on his way to the room. I slipped out a side door and rushed over to warn him about their intentions. Madiba nodded, and then said: "Leave it to me. Just stay close if I need you." I followed him as he walked into the room to greet the women who had lined up. "Aaa, goeie môre! Dis so 'n eer om u te ontmoet" (Aaah, good morning! It is an honour to meet you), he said to the first one. She froze slightly, and then went blood red.

"I am so, so honoured to meet you, Mr President. So honoured!" she blurted out in English.

The next one burst into tears. "I am so sorry what my people did to you," she cried while Madiba hugged her.

The third woman spoke to him in Zulu!

Out of the corner of my eye I spotted the leader, who had a furious expression on her face. As Madiba invited the women to tea on the stoep, he caught my eye and winked. What a master he is at these occasions, I thought.

The rest of the morning was further proof of this. His speech went down a treat, and during question time he told the most emotional stories of his time in jail. He had all the women in tears, and even though he spoke mainly Afrikaans, they all spoke English. At the end of the meeting, they gave him various gifts, including koeksisters, an Afrikaans Bible, some Afrikaans music, and photo frames for the photos of his grandchildren. It was a hugely successful morning, and in the end, through Mandela's actions, the only point that was made was his enormous capacity to turn the most hardened opponents into admirers.

# MICHAEL BAGRAIM

Representing the Cape Town Jewish community of South Africa, I had an opportunity to meet with our new democratic President, President Mandela in 1995. This was President Mandela's second year in office, and the entire country was clamouring to meet with him. Out of the blue, the South African Jewish Board of Deputies (Cape Council), received a call from President Mandela's office asking whether a few of us could meet with him, as he wanted to speak to the leadership of the Jewish community. The meeting was set for the next day in a local hotel. The request was almost surreal, and certainly readily accepted. Our boardroom in the local hotel was set and whilst everyone waited for President Mandela, I went outside to await and greet the President when he arrived. The arrival was magical, as the man immediately stepped out of the motor vehicle, unaccompanied by any sort of pomp and ceremony and without a security guard. I almost missed him.

He immediately took my hand, greeted me as a long lost friend and explained the reason for the meeting. I could feel the electricity and the greatness of the man immediately. For years we were ashamed to be South Africans, and in moments my entire perception of both South Africa and the African continent was changed. We became a proud people, and became equal in the eyes of the world. The meeting was one of the most reassuring events of my life. We as white Jewish South Africans did have a certain amount of reservations as to whether we as a people would be accepted as true and equal South Africans. This reservation melted in moments, and we were made to feel not only special, but vital to the future of our country.

# PETER STOREY

I met Nelson Mandela 50 years ago in his jail cell on Robben Island. I was a newly ordained part-time chaplain to the prison there. The guards were edgy about their new prisoners, determined to show these "terrorists" how tough they were. Sunday, when I visited, was their one day off, but it was spent in total lockdown. I was not allowed to gather them for a normal service of worship, but had to walk up and down the passageway between the cells, trying to make eye contact with each occupant, leaving him with some word of hope. One on one conversations were forbidden.

Apart from Ahmed Kathrada, who was a Muslim, the rest had all experienced mission-school education and were familiar with Christian worship. Preaching was difficult, but I tried to leave each one with a word of encouragement. Singing, however, was not bound by iron bars, and the great hymns of the church, which were well-known to them, echoed powerfully through the cell-block.

Unfortunately my security clearance was abruptly withdrawn after a few months. It was 20 years later when I next heard from Madiba. Still in prison, he used one of his precious letter-writing privileges (initially one every six months and later relaxed to slightly more often) to congratulate me on being elected to lead the Methodist Church in Southern Africa, and to express his appreciation for the care the church had shown to him through its chaplains and to his spouse Winnie in her banishment and suffering at the hands of the "system". It was in that letter that he referred to his first encounter with the Central Methodist Church in Johannesburg in the 1940's, when he was struck by the message outside: "The greatest glory in living is not in never falling, but in rising every time you fall."

In the years following his release our paths often crossed. On one of these occasions in 1994, I led a small delegation to meet with him about the crisis of guns and killing going on. Madiba came shuffling into the grand conference room next to his presidential office in Pretoria wearing an old pair of slippers. He sat down and said: "I am tired Peter. It's been a hard day, you chair the meeting please," and closed his eyes. He wasn't asleep however: at some point he looked up from the list of participating religious groups and asked: "Where are the Dutch Reformed Churches?" I said that they had been very difficult to persuade about the gun hand-in campaign. "Well," he said, "if I'm to be a patron of this, you need to get them in . . . "

In 1993 I shared a platform with Madiba and Nadine Gordimer at the centenary of Mohandas Gandhi's arrival in South Africa. On the programme were hymns sung by a Soweto church choir and Madiba began to sing quietly along with them. Gordimer seemed quite shocked and asked: "Madiba, what are you singing that stuff for?" He replied: "Ask my Bishop, Nadine. Don't you know that when I was at Fort Hare I used to go out and teach Sunday School under the trees in the veld? These are my hymns. I love them."

Madiba never left you unchanged; he was the great includer, always seeking to enlarge the circle, and in doing so, he enlarged our souls.

# ZELDA LA GRANGE

**In discussion with John Carlin.**

In August 1994, I had been working as a typist on the president's personal staff for two weeks – I ran into Madiba for the first time as I was going into his private secretary, Mary Mxadana's office to fetch a document. He came out as I entered and I shivered. By that time I had started reading a bit about him. I knew that he was a friendly man. I had seen him greeting other people, but I had never had any encounters with him. But then I ran into him by accident and he started speaking Afrikaans to me, which I didn't understand immediately because the last thing I expected was for him to speak in my own language to me. His Afrikaans was perfect but I was in such a state that I didn't understand what he was saying. I was shivering.

I was scared of him, not knowing what to expect of him, whether he was going to dismiss me, humiliate me . . . and instantly it was that feeling of guilt that all Afrikaners carry with them. Guilt, because you could see he wasn't 60, he was 75 at the time, and you could see he was old and the thing that immediately crosses your mind is: "I sent this man to jail. My people sent this man to jail! I was part of this even though I couldn't vote. I was part of this, of taking from a person like him his whole life away." I started to cry. And then he shook my hand, and he held my hand.

I was very emotional, and couldn't stop crying. It all came together, everything. Probably also not knowing – I was 23, 24 at the time – not knowing what I should do. I'd never met any president in my life. But he just held my hand and he continued to speak to me, still holding my hand, and then when he saw I was still so emotional, he put his other hand on my shoulder and said, "No, no, no . . . this is not necessary, you're overreacting a bit". I settled down, maybe smiled at that, and then he started asking me questions. Where had I grown up? What my parents did? We ended up talking for about five minutes. But it wasn't special treatment he was giving me. He would talk to all members of the staff, black and white, in the same way when he met them, asking them about their backgrounds, their families . . .

A year later, I went into his office one day to serve him tea and he said: "I want you to go to Japan with me." I didn't understand much about the mechanics of government then, to say the least, and my response was: "Thank you very much Mr President, but unfortunately I don't have money to go to Japan!" And he just burst out laughing, because I was so naive. Then he said: "No, no you go and see Professor Gerwel (the director general of the presidency), he will explain payment and protocol to you." It was obviously, as I understood later, a case of Madiba being the great strategist that he is. He knew it was important at that time to show the world we were going to embrace all cultures, we were going to have white people working with us.

# INSPIRATION

"There is no passion to
be found playing small – in
settling for a life that
is less than the one you
are capable of living."

NELSON MANDELA

# CAROLINE SMART

I was invited to attend the re-launch of the magnificent new Blue Train when it travelled to Zimbabwe in 1998.

The launch was held at Johannesburg station and headed by Nelson Mandela, then President of South Africa, and the train was to carry Deputy President Thabo Mbeki and an accompanying contingent to Zimbabwe.

I was recovering from a broken foot and had just come off the crutches so I was dependent on a walking stick.

In response to the invitation to attend the launch as a member of the media, I explained to the publicist that while I would dearly love to attend, there would be no way that I would be able to stand in the media area throughout what looked like it was going to be a fairly lengthy ceremony.

"No problem," she said. "I'll make sure you have a seat with the dignitaries." This rather daunting prospect meant that while I was greeted with smiles of welcome from the VIP's as they arrived to take their seats, there did seem an element of slight confusion as to the identity of this unknown ageing blonde in their midst!

It was a very moving launch, with Nelson Mandela giving his usual vigorous speech supporting the revival of this splendid train. After the speeches, the President and the guests walked down the station to the end of the platform to bid Thabo Mbeki and his contingent farewell.

Taking advantage of the empty space in front of me, I hobbled closer to the platform edge so that I could look through the windows of the train. Within a short space of time, the whistle blew, indicating that the train was about to leave and, with that, the full press contingent came thundering back up the platform, rushing to catch their deadlines.

Behind them, came the President's entourage, with the unmistakable Mandela figure head and shoulders above everyone else. I flattened myself against the wall to avoid getting in the way and, as he came level with me, his eye caught mine and he smiled. He moved to come across to me, but the people close to him were moving too fast. So he stopped, let them go by and came over to shake my hand.

If you've ever had your hand shaken by Nelson Mandela, you know that it is a powerful – almost bone-breaking – experience.

He asked me how I was and said he was glad to see me there. I answered something vague and he moved off. I finally found my tongue and called after him: "You're looking good, sir!" and he turned his head and the unmistakable Mandela tones came ringing back: "Thank you!"

The whole experience took no more than a minute or two but I shall never forget it. That was the day I experienced the full meaning of . . . Mandela magic!

# CLAIRE CORCORAN

It was the dawn of the new millennium when I was offered the post of Media and Information Officer at the South African Embassy, Dublin. I had just turned 25 and was extremely excited about my new career path. I had never been to South Africa before but was aware of the wealth of history, culture and beauty the country offered, all of which I was to become immersed in over the following years. And even though I was based in Ireland, I was looking forward to working on South African soil! I hit the ground running and established my office along with the help and support of my new colleagues.

It was a great surprise to me a couple of weeks later when the Head of Mission informed us all that Nelson Mandela was to visit Ireland. Imagine the effect this news had on me; I was about to meet the world renowned icon of freedom! The next few weeks flew by in a frenzy of planning and organising Madiba's visit to the Embassy. We were all totally absorbed in the process of making his trip to Dublin as memorable as possible.

Every effort was made to make his visit special. As an example, the fluorescent lighting in the corridors and conference room were replaced with ordinary lighting. This was done as a precaution against the lighting hurting Mandela's eyes which had been damaged by sunlight reflecting off the rocks in the quarry on Robben Island. Hard to imagine he had spent much of his nineteen years on the island working every day at breaking these stones and damaging his eyesight in the process. How hard it must have been for him, too, to be able to look across the ocean at Cape Town and Table Mountain just a short distance away, yet totally out of reach for him. Naturally, the Embassy building was also scoped out for any potential security risks. All this was done while we continued on with our daily tasks. The Embassy team was then briefed on the activities of the big day and, wow, what an itinerary it was! And to think I was to be a part of this! I also vividly remember Mandela's former executive personal assistant at the time, Zelda la Grange, who was a whirlwind of organisation, every 'I' had to be dotted and every 'T' crossed – and then everything checked again! In all honesty I think we were a little bit afraid of her, and secretly I was a little in awe of her!

The anticipation of his arrival grew day by day and finally I was just a few hours away from meeting him. As we all lined up in the corridor waiting to greet the great man, the sense of occasion and its importance became a reality. And finally he appeared in a flurry of activity. One of my most long-standing memories was when I first saw him and I couldn't believe how tall and strong he looked. There was also an indescribable aura of gentleness and serenity emanating from him, which is difficult to put into words to this very day. We shook hands and spoke briefly and in those few short seconds, he made you feel like you were the only person there! We all then went to the conference room to get a group photo taken. As the camera flashed, I knew this moment in time would be forever engrained in both my heart and mind. What a great honour afforded to so few. Mandela then attended various meetings and later we all went to Trinity College that evening to watch him receiving an honorary doctorate; he was conferred with a Doctor in Laws. It was also an honour for me to be part of that.

I subsequently wrote an article about the visit in the embassy magazine a couple of weeks later with the caption on the cover page entitled, 'When South African Eyes are Smiling', which was a play on words of the light hearted song, 'When Irish Eyes are Smiling'. And on reflection all these years later, that day indeed they were. In order to encapsulate how I felt about Mandela and the unforgettable day I spent in his company, here is the first verse of that song. I hope the sentiment speaks for itself.

> There's a tear in your eye and I'm wondering why,
> For it never should be there at all.
> With such power in your smile, sure a stone you'd beguile,
> So there's never a teardrop should fall,
> When your sweet lilting laughter's like some fairy song
> And your eyes twinkle bright as can be.
> You should laugh all the while and all other times smile,
> And now smile a smile for me.

Mr Mandela smiled for us that day and so did everyone who had the great pleasure of meeting him. Smiles that, in my case anyway, still linger.

# DANUTA GRAY

Why did two little boys for 10 years resist the temptation to devour two chocolates that remain, to this day, uneaten in our fridge? The chocolates are painted with portraits of Nelson Mandela, made to commemorate the award of his honorary doctorate at the National University of Ireland, Galway in 2003. I was one of the people gathered to celebrate the occasion and remember to this day the impact of his presence. He had such a wonderful energy – a serenity, a quiet strength, courage and humility that filled the room. When I returned home the boys, aged 5 and 7, spotted the chocolates and asked if they could eat them, but then paused and asked whose picture was on the front. I told them the story of Mandela, what he fought for and what a great leader he was and they then decided these chocolates were "too precious to eat". I write this as the news of Mandela's death has just been announced and recall that presence, the impact of his story on two little boys. His is a presence that will never die.

# JOHAN JANEKE

I met Mr Mandela on an aeroplane in June 1991 on the way back from London. I asked to be introduced to him and we met with a memorable handshake. I told him that Chancellor Hinderburg once said "he who controls Berlin will control Europe" and that I believed that "he who controls Soweto will control South Africa." This was shortly after his release from prison.

I felt very honoured to have met such a man of such stature. As I gave him a handshake, a photo was taken which I treasure till today as one of the most memorable moments of my life.

# ESTHER GRAUMANN

For many years I have wondered about this man, especially from a social worker's perspective. Who was he really? What made him great? What made him persevere? What traumas had he suffered? What made him remain humble and forgiving when he had every right to be arrogant and bitter? My thoughts turn to him often when I think there are too many problems and I cannot possibly make a difference in this messed-up world. A few times he has appeared in my dreams, smiling and reassuring. Whenever the news on TV showed him meeting with a celebrity, I would think "Why do they get to meet him and us ordinary South Africans don't?"

I am good friends with the well known journalist Jovial Rantao, who toured the world with Madiba following his release from prison and has written many articles from interviews with him. Sometime when we were speaking years ago, I joked with Jovial that he should "organise me tea at a certain house in Houghton"

(Mandela's residence). He said he would see what he could do. I had a fleeting moment of excitement, but then dismissed it as something that wasn't likely to happen.

One day he phoned me and said: "What are you doing at 12 tomorrow? How about taking a drive with me to Houghton?" I said: "Are you serious??" And he said: "SE-RI-OUS!" Needless to say I made sure I was free, and he picked me up from work, together with his two children, and off we went to Houghton in his sporty BMW. I had my copy of A Long Walk to Freedom to be autographed, and a letter I had written in case I had very little time to say what I wanted to say. On the way Jovial told me of his impressions of "the very special man". I asked what he thought was the greatest thing about him. He said it was his total humility and the "ability to make you feel that you are greater than he is." He advised me to speak loudly because Madiba's hearing is bad, and to turn off my camera's flash because it hurts his eyes. I asked how to address Graça Machel, and he advised me not to call her "Mrs Mandela".

We drove through the big gates and found a horde of photographers waiting for Laila Ali, the daughter of the famous boxer, who was due to arrive at 12.30. Men-in-Black with earpieces paced around, checking, checking. Everyone knew Jovial and greeted us warmly. We were asked to wait in the reception room and were offered a drink. The children bounced around and asked for juice, and I made a quick phone call to my son to find out how to switch my camera's flash off. Then Zelda la Grange emerged from the study to call us. In the passage, we paused as Jovial greeted someone else, and then I heard that unmistakeable, very famous, familiar voice calling: "Jovial, where are you? Come in! Come in!" At that point I experienced what I think could be described as a very good "trip" (not that I would know) – time slowing down, colours and shapes rushing by fast, dreams and wakefulness swirling together, and I swallowed hard to stop a few manic tears in their tracks.

We entered a beautifully furnished study. On the walls, large framed photos of Madiba with various statesmen. I looked to my left, and there he was – an old man in a large chair. My heart skipped a beat. He was smiling, as he always does, saying: "Welcome, welcome." Jovial embraced him, and the children did too. Then Jovial introduced me as "our social worker", and I said: "Mr Mandela, it is such an honour to meet you." He took my hand in both of his, and said: "Oh no, it is an honour for me to meet you!" (I've since discovered he uses this line quite often!)

We sat down, and Jovial presented him with a large, framed photograph that he had taken of Madiba on his birthday. "Good God," said Mandela, "I was handsome then!" They reminisced about the birthday celebrations, and caught up on each other's news. Jovial remarked that "Tata" was looking very well. Madiba said that he had been resting more and listening to his wife, who bosses him around. They chatted about Christmas, and Madiba had to ask Zelda to remind him where he'd been over the holidays. All the time, Zelda bustled around, pulling out chairs for us and joking with Madiba, whom she called *Khulu* (Great One or Grandfather). It is clear they have a warm and affectionate relationship. From the moment I saw him, I noticed nothing else in the room. I wish I could return and look at all the pictures, photos, artefacts. I wish I could browse through the books on the shelves and walk on the rugs. I'd like to look out of the windows into the gardens, and take note of what sort of curtains frame them. But all I saw was that wide smile and straight, strong teeth; his much whiter hair; his full lip; his light-damaged eyes; his frail body beneath another beautiful hand-made *Madiba* shirt; his surprisingly youthful hands; the way he pulls his bottom lip down when he says his characteristic "aaah" between sentences.

"Let's take some pictures!" The children sprang into position. Jovial, Zelda and I tried to take decent photos quickly and without the flash. There was much merriment and small talk. As I knelt down beside him, he took my hand and Jovial joked that Madiba always smiles more broadly when he has a lady beside him. I was aware of the warmth of his hand and the sound of his chuckling under his breath.

I put his autobiography down before him and jokingly asked "Madiba, do you remember this book?" "Aah yes, I've heard about it" he joked back, "I think it was written by some terrorist?" He signed his name simply, with a trembling hand, only one word: "Mandela". I asked him what advice he would give to this social worker who has many hills to climb (borrowing a phrase from his book). He asked me to repeat the question, and then became distracted by the photo on the wall behind me.

"I'm just noticing that photo. Why was I so gloomy there? What was I doing?"

Zelda said: "You were discussing the state of the nation."

"Oh, was I?"

"No," she laughed, "I don't know what you were doing, Khulu."

"I look so gloomy."

I remembered my letter just as we were saying our goodbyes. As the others left, I presented it to Madiba. Opening the envelope, his humour returned: "I hope this isn't a letter of demand?"

"No, a letter of admiration!" I replied.

"Oh! For me?"

On the way out we passed his daughter Zindzi and Laila with her American entourage, all in gold chains and Ray Bans, in the passage. We stepped outside, the photographers and camera crew swung around, only to see it was nobody special.

It took me two days to come down to earth. Everyone at work was very patient with me, a bit like I imagine a village would tolerate their ever-smiling idiot. I told a friend that I felt as if God, or the universe, or something big had acknowledged me (yes, ridiculous, but that's how it felt.)

That afternoon, a cleaner stared at my photos in disbelief. "Miss Esther! Is that YOU? With MADIBA??" He clapped his hands, genuinely sharing in my delight. He said: "You know, Miss Esther, when you meet a man like that? It is really God blessing you."

# GISELLE COURTNEY

Madiba paid a visit to the SA Mint in Midrand in 1996. I was there to take photos for my newly founded independent community newspaper, the *Midrand Mirror*. To my consternation us journalists were told we were not allowed to use flash photography as it hurt Madiba's eyes. This was a result of the years he had toiled in the limestone mine on Robben Island. I panicked as the film in my camera was not the right ASA and I expected the photos to be dark and unusable. But the Madiba Magic was at work . . . every photograph came out beautifully and we published a front-page photo of Madiba with a beaming young lady who worked at the mint. What a gift it was to begin our newspaper with the image of this era's Rainmaker and be touched so tangibly by the Madiba Magic!

# HUGH FLYNN

I am currently the CEO of ASL Aviation Group. I've never had the privilege of meeting Nelson Mandela in person, but was thrilled along with a handful of aspring pilots to see him wave at us through the window of a South African Air Force VIP HS125 aircraft.

At the time I was a part time flight instructor at the Swartkops Air Force Base. On an early Saturday morning back in 1996, while we were readying to commence flying activities, this twin engine jet taxied past a number of us on the flight apron.

The pilot of the twin enjin jet, (a HS125), whose son was undergoing flying training at the Defence Flying Club at Swartkops, knew us. He specially slowed his aircraft and pointed backwards where we could see an old man smiling and waving enthusiastically at us! We realised it was the great man. It was Nelson Mandela!

The impression that wave left on a handful of people, is indescribable.

# JAN BEZUIDENHOUT

In January 1998 Nelson Mandela (during a holi-day break from his work as then President of South Africa) reached out to a group of young volunteers who were on a work camp to renovate a school in Mozambique. The Southern African Student Volunteers (sasvo) arranged work camps for volunteers from diverse backgrounds to renovate and build schools in Southern Africa. Some of their projects were funded by the Nelson Mandela Children's Fund (nmcf). In 1996 they entered into a reciprocal agreement with the South African High Commission (sahc) in Maputo. If they could provide a young intern to work and learn more about development on a small business development project (of the sahc), he/she could then also arrange the first sasvo work camps in Mozambique. This is the story of how Jan Bezuidenhout, the sasvo seconded intern and the group of student volunteers he coordinated to do a work camp met with Nelson Mandela:

"I just came back from a year of backpacking and working on

farms, restaurants and pubs in England and Scotland and met with a SASVO co-ordinator Jacob van Garderen, (now director of Lawyers for Human Rights) at "Oom Gert se Plek" (a coffee shop/bar on the University of Pretoria campus). He mentioned that they were looking for someone to do a short stint as an intern at the SAHC in Maputo and also arrange the SASVO work camps.

My application had been successful and (besides meeting Nelson Mandela while I was there!) I was privileged to go and live and work in Maputo for about a year during 1997/1998. Months of prep work went into the work camp arrangements and I was very excited to receive the South African volunteers, who came by train to Maputo during the university holidays in January 1998. After collecting them at the train station I took them to lunch. As an employee of the SAHC I received a monthly entertainment allowance. At that age, I didn't really know much about wining and dining so I never used it, but when the volunteers arrived I thought it would be appropriate to take them all for lunch at a restaurant. Some of them were not shy and ordered the most expensive items on the menu so I blew almost the whole allowance in one day!

The work camp had been going well and I told Judy Greathead, the development attaché whom I reported to, that some of the South African students requested to meet with the high commissioner. She didn't look all that enthusiastic, but a couple of days later she called me in and said that they should come to the presidential guest house on the last Sunday of their three weeks in Mozambique. Nelson Mandela was there on a short break with Graça Machel, he knows about the Southern African Student Volunteers (we were partly funded by the Nelson Mandela Children's Fund) and he would love to meet with our team!

She asked me not to tell the students where they will be going or whom they will meet so I just told them to be ready on the Sunday to come with me to meet someone important. On the day I couldn't hold it any longer and when they got into the twin cab pick-up truck I broke the news: it was chaos! There were two guys in the back and they helped to bounce the pick-up truck along with the rhythm of the singing as we drove the last kilometre or so down the streets of Maputo's upmarket Sommerschield neighbourhood. At the presidential guest house the guards, who had to do the security check upon our arrival, couldn't hold back their smiles at the pick-up truck full of ululating students.

My preconceived idea was that we would just meet with him and then be off again. Reality was much different: we were taken to the lounge to sit down. We waited for about 10 minutes (dead quiet). I will never forget the moment when we heard his voice (in conversation with Judy and the high commissioner) as he came walking down the hallway. Somehow I never thought that I would first **hear** Nelson Mandela and then physically see him a few seconds later. Just the sound of his voice switched on the energy in the room and everyone got up automatically (almost like the crowd at a rugby match when a try is about to be scored). He first met and greeted each of us personally, (I struggled to get words out) one of the students had been in Umkontho we Sizwe in Angola and others had mutual acquaintances with him in the Eastern Cape so it took a while before we sat down as conversations started to flow during the introductions. It felt like we were visitors of the family: a beaming Graça Machel and her two daughters were serving up the tea and biscuits, no servants or waiters.

Nelson Mandela then spoke with us for about half an hour,

much of it I can't remember as my mind was going all over the place. What I do recall was that he was very proud to be associated with our organisation. In those years we were one of the few youth organisations at universities in South Africa that managed to draw young people from across the whole spectrum of South African society. Other multi-racial student organisations existed of course, but didn't manage to draw the same kinds of numbers in diversity. Students on our work camps were working side by side with community volunteers, mixing sweat with earth, to build and renovate schools all over southern Africa. Makarere University in Uganda also had a very active SASVO branch – the idea was always to drop the *Southern* and *Students* from the name and just make it African Volunteers or AVO. (Unfortunately the organisation might have grown too big too fast and when the funding dried up SASVO also gradually came to an end).

At the conclusion of tea and discussions, we went outside on the veranda to take a group picture. I felt embarrassed as some of the students brought their own cameras along and started manoeuvring him around to have their individual pictures taken, i.e. "now stand like this with me and my girlfriend." He wasn't fazed and after a while he came up to me and asked: "And you, don't you also want to have a picture with me?" I stuttered: "Of course, but I don't want to inconvenience you". He then just smiled and pulled me in by the arm, along with Kgomotso (University of Pretoria) and Matthew (University of the Witwatersrand), who were also a bit less forward in their need for pictures, to have my most prized picture ever taken.

Besides the fact that we had all been inspired by Nelson Mandela's mere presence we had the best work camp ever. The way that we were received, as guests of the family, Nelson Mandela's emphasis and appreciation for an attempt by our student volunteer organisation to bring people closer to each other as well as the fact that he reached out to me, when he saw that I was taken aback a bit by the situation, will be with me for life. I am not usually a quiet person myself, but I have often later on found that you have to ensure that those who are standing back, whilst others are grabbing the space, also get their chance to have their say and make a contribution. No **direct** correlation to our situation with the pictures, but if we always only listen to those who shout the loudest, we may miss out on the most creative and innovative ideas that could make us progress to greater unity and inclusivity."

# MARGARETHA BARNARD

I had two choices: go as fast as possible until the cacophony of rattling parts in the car did not keep rhythm with the involuntary movements of my innards, or go at a dung beetle pace which did not stop the dust downpour nor sooth my crushed coccyx.

There is no secret recipe for driving on a corrugated road. You just have to grind on the dust between your teeth and do it.

My job at Namibia's largest daily newspaper took me to all kinds of places, but I loved following leads on bumpy roads far away from civilisation where deadlines disappeared in the sand.

With the sun storming the western horizon like a desert elephant smelling water, I had to reach camp before dusk to avoid crossing paths with one of these giants in the dark.

The aim of my visit was not to track desert elephants, but to follow a good news story of rural communities who had started to manage their natural resources by forming conservancies.

There was an abundance of stories around the desert campfire the first night. When I looked up I felt myself evaporating into the infinity of the glittering sky. I came back to earth like a shooting star when a man stepped out of the dark into the fire circle shaking my hand in congratulations on the prize I had won shortly before.

He recognised me from a photo in the newspaper where I sat next to Nelson Mandela as one of the 13 category winners in the CNN African Journalist of the Year competition.

The memory of meeting Madiba was as beautiful as the night sky, but later that night it was the power of the media in reaching such remote parts of the world that left me astonished.

As I found myself negotiating bumps again poking through my thin camp mattress, I could not begin to imagine what 27 years in jail must have been like. I felt immensely privileged to have met the man who had survived such suffering.

I still ached at the thought of how for the first time in my career as a journalist I could not think of any questions to ask or quirky remarks to make, despite sitting next to Mandela for a photograph.

Like a true politician, Mandela on the other hand never appears to be at a loss for words. As he met each of the winners from all over Africa he had something to say or he asked a question about each individual's country, current politics and its people.

In his speech he focused on the responsibility journalists have in reporting the news. Although his message was still fresh in my mind, it was only on my return home when every thud and knock resulting from the corrugation jolted me into a realisation of how his words had transformed into a profound life lesson for me around a faraway desert campfire.

# MAX DU PREEZ

Nelson Mandela played a role in my life for a long time. I went to study law at the insistence of my father – he said I could one day be as great a lawyer as Percy Yutar, the prosecutor who presented the State's case at the Rivonia Trial years earlier that saw Mandela go to jail for a long time.

I remember reading a book on the trial to figure out why Yutar was such a hero. It painted Mandela and his co-accused as dangerous communist terrorists and I felt a sense of relief that these enemies of my people were now on Robben Island.

But I also remember wondering as a platteland teenager why Mandela was prepared to die for a cause that my society at the time saw as treasonous and unchristian. Could it just be that my father and the leaders of Afrikanerdom were misrepresenting his cause? My father was angry when I asked him.

I was reminded of this when as a cub reporter in Soweto on June 16, 1976, I was faced with black teenagers challenging the police to shoot them. I knew then that there was something I wasn't getting.

In 1984 I interviewed a Swapo leader who had just been released from Robben Island where he had served many years with Mandela – Andimba Toivo ya Toivo.

He wanted to talk about Namibia, I wanted to interrogate him about Mandela.

By this time, I had had a different exposure as a journalist to what apartheid really meant. After my conversation with Toivo ya Toivo I knew that my country's prospects for peace and freedom were tied in with the fate of Mandela. Late in 1988 I wrote Mandela an open letter in the newspaper I was then editing, Vrye Weekblad – I knew he was a subscriber in jail.

I asked him to liberate Afrikaners also when he did come out of jail to help establish a proper democracy in South Africa.

A few days after his release in February 1990, Mandela phoned me to invite me to his home in Soweto. He came out to my car with an outstretched hand and greeted me in Afrikaans.

He poured me tea and explained that he wanted to apologise for not responding to my open letter, but the prison authorities wouldn't allow him to send it to me.

Mandela apologised for his "Xhosa accent" when speaking Afrikaans and told me about his vision of a united, free and fair – and non-racial – South Africa.

By this time I had interviewed most political leaders in South Africa as well as several African and Western prime ministers and presidents. This man was very, very different.

He had an aura of moral authority about him, he had a clear vision, he had no doubt about his calling to deliver freedom and dignity to the last country in the world where white people ruled over black people. But he wasn't all politician, he was a proper mensch.

I interviewed Mandela several times as president and after he retired and had two private meetings with him. He was fundamentally the same person I met in February 1990.

Three years ago, the London-based publishers of the *Rough Guides* books asked me to write *The Rough Guide to Nelson Mandela*, a book that was published last year. I spent two years researching his life before, during and after Robben Island. Last year, I made an hour-long documentary on his life for the Afrikaans TV channel KykNet.

During this deep research I came across many of Mandela's weaknesses and mistakes, all of which I documented in the book.

Rather than seeing a hero with feet of clay, it reaffirmed my view of what a special human being he was. He wasn't a saint sent by some higher being after all; he was an African and South African of flesh and blood, a product of our history and society.

Yes, Mandela was the almost messianic figure that had facilitated the improbable transition from apartheid and white rule to an open democracy and sold a new order to white South Africans after 300 years of colonialism and 50 years of apartheid.

But let's not forget that he was also, with Walter Sisulu, responsible for reinvigorating and modernising the almost dormant ANC in the 1950s.

To me, Mandela was living proof that good can prevail over evil, that there actually is something such as a shared humanity.

# MICHAEL DE HAAST

In June 2003, I was fortunate enough to meet Nelson Mandela, since I was instrumental in bringing him to Galway, Ireland. Following Madiba's receipt of an honorary Doctorate conferred on him by the National University of Galway, he arrived at the Radisson Blu Hotel (of which I was the General Manager) with the South African Ambassador Melanie Verwoerd. I escorted the President to his suite and on learning that I was a fellow South African and co-host of the evening's fundraising banquet, he invited me to sit and have refreshments with him and the Ambassador. We spent a good thirty minutes with Madiba in the Presidential Suite and this turned out to be a life changing experience for me.

What struck me most was his aura and calmness – the three of us "chatting" as if we were friends, sitting at home. Madiba asked me about my reasons for leaving South Africa and wanted to know if I had been accepted by the Irish people, to which I answered that I had been transferred through my work as a Hotel

GM, and that the Irish had accepted us as a family into their community, albeit probably fast-tracked, as a result of our involvement in sponsorship to all the local sporting teams and community upliftment initiatives. We spoke about The Corrs (the band playing at the gala dinner to be held later that night in his honour) and his love for Irish music. He asked me about my opinion of the Celtic Tiger and talked about the Special Olympics, his love of sport, and his decision to attend the Rugby World Cup Final of 1995. We went on to discuss the effect that winning the title of World Champions had on South Africa as a nation. His interaction with me was so authentic and humble that I was completely put at ease by his nature and reassuring manner – he made me feel like an equal and an old friend.

One of my mantras in life is the following: Self-Control is strength; right thoughts is mastery and calmness is power. To me, President Nelson Mandela is the epitome of calmness. Thank You, Madiba, for having such a profound effect on my life!

# OWEN SIMONS

Sunday, 11th February 1990 is etched in my memory forever.

I heard on radio that Nelson Rolihlahla Mandela was to be released from Victor Verster prison, and that he was going to address his people at City Hall. Jubilation!! Here was a man who had sacrificed his freedom and family, as a matter of principle despite the consequences, consequences that were unimaginable to many of us in this country.

My first view of this great man was when he emerged from Victor Verster Prison . . . lean, proud and upright, as he held hands with Ma Winnie. I was giddy with excitement and wonder, and thought that my heart would burst. If it did, I would die happy. At the time I was watching his release on TV, about 25 kilometers away in Cape Town's Cape Flats. I saw the press' excited reaction. At one point I saw Leon Muller, a photographer and colleague at the Argus, in a tree to get a better shot of Madiba.

I knew at that moment that I had to go into town to be part of things. I promptly found myself on the train to Cape Town. I could not get there fast enough. The trip took about 40 minutes. I was employed as a Library Assistant at the the Argus Newspaper at the time.

On my way into town, and while in town, the air was filled with excitement and Madiba's name even though the convoy had not yet made its way to the center of Cape Town. Upon my arrival at the Grand Parade, I was engulfed in the euphoria. On everyone's lips was the fact that Madida was so tall – most people had by that time seen his release on TV. A more beautifully historic day would be hard to find.

By that time, I had under my belt a few big marches, including one of about 30 000 people, in September 1989, in which Archbishop Tutu, Dr. Alan Boesak, Gordon Olivier, Sheikh Nazeem Mohammed and others had taken part in. So as a "mass march" veteran, I skillfully edged my way onto Darling Street, which is practically on the edge of City Hall. That was as far as I could jostle to.

Then we waited and waited.

Then he was there! Nelson Mandela stood practically in front of me! Oh, how I envied those entrepreneurial fellas who clambered **right up** to the balcony, and stood right next to Madiba! Either way, I could see the expressions of his face.

Then, holding our breaths we waited for his first words.

Then he spoke! His voice was strong, clear and fantastically mellifluous at the same time. The crowd went wild. Tears were streaming down my face; around me there was not a dry eye in sight.

And Madiba continued, pulling us all into the euphoria of that God-given day. I certainly felt as if I was on a cloud.

WOW!

# QUINTUS
# VAN DER MERWE

As diplomat in charge of the French Desk at the SA Department of Foreign Affairs, I was privileged to accompany President Mandela on an official visit to France in July 1996. We were only a small group of South Africans, including Rusty Evans, DG of Foreign Affairs; Alec Erwin, Minister of Commerce and Industry; Jakes Gerwel, head of the President's office; Zelda la Grange, the President's personal assistant; his doctor and security officials.

As a member of the advance party I left early and three days later awaited President Mandela at the airport. When we were introduced to him, he walked towards me with a broad smile. I introduced myself, and when he heard that my surname was Van der Merwe, he took my hand, placed his other hand on my shoulder and addressed me in Afrikaans with: "Dis 'n voorreg om U te ontmoet, Meneer van der Merwe." (It's a privilege to meet you, Mr van der Merwe).

After that I stayed with him in the Elysee Palace in Paris as official guests of the French government and joined him in cavalcades speeding through the streets. We attended the French National Day and several other meetings. We also visited the apartment where Dulcie September was shot. Throughout I was impressed with his sense of humour and friendliness and the trouble he took to talk to ordinary people and make jokes. At night, I helped Zelda la Grange and one of his bodyguards to put his mattress on the floor. July is hot in Paris and I was told he preferred to put his mattress on the floor, as he believed that this prevented the French mosquitoes from biting him.

Every year on Bastille Day the President of France invites 2000 promising young people to his residence for a garden party. Nelson Mandela was President Chirac's guest. When President Chirac appeared in the summery garden, there was the expected, polite applause, but when President Mandela appeared, total chaos erupted. It was as if the Messiah had appeared in the garden, and the security personnel and I had our hands full to prevent the almost hysterical admirers from knocking Mandela down. While a few of us formed a small protective circle around him, he laughingly touched the many outstretched hands over our heads for several minutes, while a somewhat flustered President Chirac tried unsuccessfully over the microphone to restore order. I also heard Mandela regularly utter his well-known "How are you?" and a few times even "Merci".

In a conversation later between the two presidents, Mandela called for the remains of Saartjie Baartman to be repatriated to South Africa. This took place shortly after the visit.

# TRISH LOMBARD

I was cabin crew for SAA and shortly after Mr Mandela's release from jail ,he and Winnie and a "shadow cabinet" travelled to Rio/Buenos Aires. I had the great good fortune of looking after the Mandelas who were quiet and unassuming and just wonderful. Of course we did not have the usual aeroplane conversations – "chicken or beef", since he and Winnie were in first class.

In fact they were the only ones sitting downstairs in first class – the rest of the inner circle were upstairs in the smoking section of first class, but there was lots of to-ing and fro-ing between the upstairs and the business class where the security guards and others were seated. We repeatedly had to turn them away so that they would leave Mr Mandela in peace – and I remember a copious quantity of whisky being consumed by them all, but not by Mr Mandela

When the cabin lights were eventually dimmed for the night

and Mr Mandela was getting comfortable, I had to kneel at his feet and help him remove his shoes as he was struggling a bit! It was such a wonderful moment and something I will never forget.

# KINDNESS

"I believe that in
the end it is kindness and
generous accommodation
that are the catalysts
for real change"

NELSON MANDELA

# ALLYSON NEIDER-HOFFMAN

Rev. André Scheffler was for many years a member of the board of the Noluthando School for the Deaf in Khayelitsha, Cape Town. He told me once how he had, as part of his duties as a member of the clergy, visited Robben Island to minister to the convicts detained there and Madiba was one of them. They became too "close" according to the Apartheid authorities. On one of Rev. Scheffler's trips to the island Madiba gave him a guava to give to his wife, who had a cold. Rev. Scheffler was touched that an inmate who had so little could give away something so valuable to him. On leaving the island Rev. Scheffler was searched and the guava was found and confiscated. Rev. Scheffler was then banned from returning to the island to minister to the inmates. In later years Madiba told Rev. Scheffler that he thought the "old man" had died when he didn't return to visit them.

# ANDY BOLNICK

For as long as I can remember Nelson Mandela was part of my consciousness. I grew up in a family that was very politically and socially aware and who believed in social justice. I think it came from our Jewish heritage – from being oppressed for so many years and also more recently, the Holocaust. And so my mother and father very much incalcated in all of us the values to fight against political and social injustice and the understanding that we could not sit around and do nothing. My mother was in Black Sash and I went with her into the townships and saw black children as my friends and equals. My father also had many people working for him and they all lived on our property. It was like a little kibbutz.

But it meant that we were seen as different and when I would play with white children there was a lot of prejudice towards me. That became my struggle. Unlike the other white kids, I can remember that as young as age 4 and 5, I knew about Mandela and that he was imprisoned for his beliefs. I had quite a vivid imagination and played out these elaborate scenarios. We lived in Houghton (close to where Madiba would eventually live) and I would sit in the attic and imagine that our entire roof housed a secret special operation or military wing against apartheid. I would fantasize how I would assist in Nelson Mandela's escape or rescue from prison.

I eventually outgrew those imaginings, but as my family's involvement in the struggle grew, my brother was eventually detained and upon his release had to flee abroad. During that time when we were on holiday in Cape Town, I would look down from Lions' Head towards Robben Island and be filled with such sadness, thinking if I can only get over the sea I could not only get to Mandela, but also to my brother whom I so missed.

It was only when I was about 17 or 18 years old that I found out that I shared the same birthday as Mandela. In 1990 on the day of his release I was overseas. I was desperately sad that I wasn't back home and I walked around with a radio glued to my ear and recorded the commentary of the moment of his release. "Nelson Mandela on the steps of Victor Verster prison and his hand goes up . . . " I taped it about a 100 times. The tears just flowed when I heard his speech at the Cape Town parade. When he said: "I greet you not as a prophet . . . " and he said what he said I was just elated that my hero, who I had believed in for all these years was finally free and was clearly going to live up to all we had always dreamt he would be and more.

In 1993, after returning to South Africa, I wanted to give Madiba a birthday present. I was selling shoes at the time and found out from his PA, Zelda la Grange, he wore a size 9. I then got the most beautiful pair I could lay my hands on. The shoes were very intricately woven, in a beautiful tan colour. Instead of a birthday card, I decided to write him a message on the soles of the shoes. I told him how I live close to him and that he had been my hero and alluded to the huge role that he was about to step into as president of South Africa. I also think I said something corny like: "if the shoe fits, wear it".

Two years later, in 1995 with Madiba now president, we still lived quite close to his house. On our collective birthday I took an early walk with my mum. As we passed Madiba's house, I showed my ID book to the guards at the gates to prove that I shared a birthday with Madiba. On the spur of the moment, I then asked if I could possibly wish him a happy birthday. I also mentioned the fact that I had sent him the shoes two years earlier and one of his bodyguards said: "I remember those shoes! Madiba showed them to us."

They said they would phone and ask. We waited, not thinking for a moment that we would really be allowed to go in. But then the message came – "Madiba says send her in". My mum insisted that I go in on my own, so I walked apprehensively toward the house and through the front door. Someone met me there and asked me to sit on a small bench at the bottom of the stairs. They said that Madiba was just getting ready and that he would come down in a moment. The next moment I heard his footsteps as he was coming down the stairs. I could see up towards the landing where there was this magnificent stained glass window with the most beautiful colours. As Madiba came into sight and turned on the landing, the light from the stain glass window surrounded him. He was wearing one of his lovely golden shirts and with the light around him, it was just an astonishing image.

He came slowly down the stairs and said: "I hear it is your birthday." He embraced me tightly and then wished me a happy birthday. Of course I wished him a happy birthday back and then he asked me about what work I was doing. I told him about my family and their political involvement, but I felt a little sad, that I could not say that I was following my heart and working with communities and for social justice; something that would change after our meeting.

In the end we most probably only chatted for a few minutes, but it felt like an eternity being in his presence. It was just such a special, amazing thing to be with him on my own and for him to ask me what was going on in my life. The best birthday present any one can ask for.

Eventually someone came to say that he had to meet with his family who was there to celebrate his birthday.

He embraced me again and then slowly walked away.

# FRANCOIS VAN HOOGSTRATEN

In 1991, I was playing squash for the South African Defense Force team in Durban. It was early July and our team was fortunate enough to be staying at the Elangeni Hotel on the beachfront. At the same time the Gunston 500 surfing competition was also being held at North Beach. In addition a big ANC conference was being hosted at the Elangeni and Maharani Hotels.

My best friend from high school, Miles, was competing in the surfing competition. Being eighteen years old we were very short of money, so I had offered him a space on the floor of my hotel room.

One evening we were making our way back to the Elangeni Hotel, struggling to carry wetsuits, surfboards and lots of other gear. With the hotel being very busy there was a long wait at the lift. My friend Miles ran off to the toilet on the ground floor leaving me with all the gear in front of the lift. I was looking at a group of around 6-8 people walking towards the lift, when I realised to my shock that it was Madiba, Winnie Mandela and a few bodyguards!

Once I recognised them I became nervous, not only because it was them, but I kept thinking about the fact that I was sneaking my friend up into the hotel without him really being allowed. Thankfully he was still in the loo.

In the mean time, I frantically started to pick up things in order to make the area clear for them to get past me into the lift. As they got to the lift Madiba greeted me and asked what sport I was playing. Still trying to get the squash bags, surfboards etc. together I was so nervous, I couldn't even answer.

As the doors of the lift opened, all the bodyguards stepped into the lift, but Madiba waited patiently while I struggled with the gear. To my great surprise he suddenly put his hand out for me to give him a bag, so I could get the rest of the stuff into the lift! Only once all the gear and I were inside did he get in.

My friend still hadn't arrived, but I happily left him behind. After all, I was in the lift a foot from Nelson Mandela, going up to the 6th floor!

As the doors opened on my floor, Madiba asked a bodyguard to help me get all my stuff out. He again waited patiently and even joked with me that he would never venture out into the ocean in a silly wetsuit and on a little board like that.

All I could do was to thank him. As I walked down the passage with the biggest grin on my face, I turned and looked back. With the lift doors closing Madiba gave me a wave goodbye.

When my friend Miles got back to the room he was amazed that I managed to get everything to the room on my own. Then I told him what had happened and he was simply blown away.

I was only eighteen years old, but it is a few minutes in my life that I will never forget. What amazed me most was that he, Nelson Mandela, put his hand out and physically helped me to carry my bags, when no one else did.

# GLYNN KATZIN

My late Dad was Kitt Katzin – he was an investigative journalist for the Sunday Star, previous to that he worked for the Saturday Star and the Sunday Express. He was well known in journalistic circles having uncovered/investigated amongst others, the Smit murders, the Info Scandal, the Matric Scandal, the Helderberg disaster, and won numerous awards during his career, not to mention being extremely unpopular with the then government, especially PW Botha.

In April 1991, he was in hospital where he had an operation to lengthen his life by a few months as he had pancreatic cancer. At the same time he was announced as one of three nominees, together with Radio 702 and the Naidoo family, for a human rights award and this was making some news in the press and on radio.

I remember him taking calls and doing interviews from his hospital bed. During one of the calls, someone said: "Please hold for Mr Mandela", and the next thing Madiba was on the line. Madiba wished my dad well with his health and congratulated him on his nomination. But the thing that made my dad's day was that Madiba said to him that when he was on Robben Island, he was allowed one newspaper a week. He told my dad that he chose *his* newspaper so he could read *his* articles.

This call from Madiba was made against the backdrop of him having been out of prison for a short time, he was under siege from the world's press wherever he went, as well as trying to lead South Africa to a peaceful solution. Yet, he still had taken the time to make that call to Dad.

Sadly my Dad passed away in December 1991 and never got to see South Africa becoming a democracy. Wherever my dad is right now, I bet you he's still smiling from that call.

# SHIRLEY NAIDOO

In 2008 I was asked to come for an interview for the position of housekeeper, with Madiba and Mrs. Machel. I was very scared, so scared that I really did not want the job, so I kept giving them negative answers, thinking that I would not get the job. Despite it being a very informal chat, I was just petrified as you can imagine. At the end of the interview Madiba asked me where I am working now and when would I want to start were I to be employed by him. I answered: "Well, Mr Mandela I can only start four months from now, in April, since I have been working for my boss for 10 years. It is now the December holiday season so it is very busy and I can't just leave him." Imagine saying that to Nelson Mandela! I thought that would for sure mean I would not get the job, but to the contrary. I think he liked the answer, because he said: "You are very loyal to your boss and I hope when you work for me, you will be just as loyal. Ok, I will wait for you."

Of course when I went back to my boss and told him that I got this job with Nelson Mandela, he graciously said that I could finish in mid-January. So I started with Mr Mandela in February. It was a chaotic time, with the opening of parliament soon after I started, but thankfully after one week, Mr Mandela said that I did not have to go through the normal three-month probation period and that I was appointed permanently as his housekeeper.

And so my life changed as I was privileged to serve this extraordinary man.

# LEADERSHIP

"It is better to lead from behind
and to put others in front,
especially when you celebrate
victory when nice things occur.
You take the front line when
there is danger. Then people will
appreciate your leadership."

"There are times when a leader
must move out ahead of the
flock, go off in a new direction,
confident that he is leading his
people the right way."

NELSON MANDELA

# AHMED KATHRADA

You can't categorise Nelson Mandela as you would your next-door neighbour, or fit him into the ordinary person we know. One can use a lot of adjectives . . . courage, foresight, compassion, calmness, diplomacy, patience, tolerance, magnanimity, discipline, loyalty . . .

But I would single out courage and foresight.

It was after he had been separated from us at Pollsmoor Prison that he took the initiative in starting the negotiation process. That required courage and foresight. Here he was, not able to liaise with anybody, not with us, not with the organisation outside. And he knew that what he was doing might expose him to criticism. And as we discovered later, there were some elements who said he was selling out. By that time he had managed to send a message to Oliver Tambo.

But he said: "There comes a time when a leader has to lead."

Some of these qualities evolved as a result of experience. He was a leader of the ANC Youth League in 1950 when the alliance organisations, the Transvaal ANC, the Indian Congress and the Communist Party, took a decision to go on strike. The youth league was opposed to the strike action because it was exclusionist and anti-communist, and did not want to take part in cooperation with other organisations. Mandela at that time was bent on breaking up pro-strike meetings. He physically pulled a speaker, Yusuf Cachalia, from the platform. I, all of 21 at the time, argued with him about it and he took it very badly.

But when the strike was successful he had the bigness to acknowledge that he was wrong in opposing it, and he acknowledged that pulling Cachalia from the platform was not the correct thing to do. He was always open to persuasion.

When [apartheid bantustan leader] Kaiser Matanzima wanted to visit him in prison, he, being a democrat, and sometimes exasperatingly so, wanted to consult with all of us. He was close to Matanzima as a relative, and also very grateful for what Matanzima had done in preparing his mother's funeral, and he wanted to thank him. He put it to the ANC people and stood his ground. But when he found that the majority was against the visit, he acceded to the majority.

# GERRY ADAMS

The green rolling grasslands of Qunu were coming alive in the early morning dawn light as I climbed down off the bus. It had been a three-and-a half-hour journey from the airport at East London, in the Eastern Cape, along dark and twisting roads. Qunu is Madiba's home and it is where he chose to be buried.

As the sun slowly lifted itself above the hills, its light revealed a landscape similar to others I have seen in the west of Ireland. A big blue sky and distant homes scattered across hills. It was here that Madiba was born and had grown up. And it was to Qunu he returned. He was home with his clan after nine days of national mourning in South Africa.

It was an emotional visit, a deeply sad moment. The day before the funeral I had attended the ANC's "sending off" event at Waterkloof air force base. I was greatly honoured when asked to participate in this and to stand as part of the guard of honour over Madiba's remains.

I first saw Nelson Mandela when he visited Dublin in 1990. That was the day the Irish soccer team returned home. And when Madiba appeared, a section of the crowd began to chant "Ooh ahh Paul Mc Grath's Da"– Paul McGrath was the only black player on the Irish team. So, the good humour of Ireland shone through.

In 1995, the year after the IRA cessation and before all-party negotiations had commenced in the Irish peace process, I travelled to South Africa with comrades at the invitation of the ANC to speak to senior figures who had been centrally involved in the process of negotiations.

That was when I met Madiba for the first time. I was delighted to be meeting with one of my heroes.

During the conflict there was a close working relationship between Irish republicans and the ANC. The late Kader Asmal who did tremendous work in the leadership of the Irish anti-apartheid movement, along with his wife Louise, tells in his autobiography how the IRA provided practical training and advice and assistance with military operations to MK.

Kader says that the famous attack of May 31st 1980 on the Sasol Oil Refinery near Johannesburg was carried out with the assistance of the Irish Republican Army.

Walter Sisulu, Cyril Ramaphosa, Thabo Mbeki, Ronnie Kasrils and many others who were in the leadership of the ANC were pleased to remember the long commitment, as was Madiba himself, of Irish republicans to their cause. In jail for those decades, on Robben Island, Madiba maintained his international perspective and his interest in the struggle in Ireland.

In his cell, in common with all political prisoners, he was allowed as a privilege a calendar on which he marked significant events. On the 5th May 1981 a simple single line is written: "*IRA martyr*

*Bobby Sands dies."* A tribute, handwritten, on a paper calendar on a cell wall in South Africa which recognises the bond of those who struggle for justice.

In our conversations with Madiba we found him funny, self-effacing, modest, totally relaxed and very focused. He was also very tough, stubborn, determined and committed as he needed to be to survive apartheid; to survive over two and a half decades in prison with hard labour.

He was immovable on core principles, on core values, on core issues but pragmatic on tactics and other matters.

It is also interesting that the British government at the time lobbied hard for Madiba not to meet me. And when it was clear that the ANC and Madiba were determined that the visit should go ahead, the British lobbied for no handshake or photograph. He ignored them.

I was privileged and deeply honoured to meet Madiba many times after that; in South Africa, in Ireland and in Britain. He was always hugely supportive of the Irish peace process. He had an enormous depth of understanding of the twists and turns of our process. And he knew there was an onus on governments, as well as those involved in struggle, to resolve issues.

Despite his age and when I last met with him, despite his increased physical frailty, his mind was as sharp as a razor; conversant with world affairs and with the affairs of his own continent, with for example the injustice of the wars in Iraq or Afghanistan.

Nelson Mandela was a very remarkable human being. In death as in life he will continue to inspire and encourage oppressed peoples everywhere. And in that way his legacy will live on.

Madiba was a leader who by his courage demonstrated that it is possible to reconcile differences.

By his example he showed us that it is possible to build peace out of conflict; something we try to do on our own island; and that a better and more equal future based on fairness is possible, and that unity can be forged out of division.

He was a Freedom Fighter, a political prisoner, a negotiator, a healer, a peacemaker, a father, a grandfather and a husband. He was a friend to those engaged in the struggle for justice across the globe.

He believed in Ubuntu (we are all interconnected and a person cannot exist separate from society; we all have responsibilities to each other).

At the end of the funeral ceremony in Qunu, Madiba's remains were placed in the earth. The language was different and the hymns unfamiliar but as family members placed a flower in the grave and took some dirt to drop in on the coffin the similarities with our own funeral experience in Ireland were obvious.

Madiba's grave is on top of the hillside where a small garden has been built. It has a magnificent view of Qunu and of the hills where Madiba played as a boy.

Madiba is gone. But his words are all around us. The legacy of hope and courage and forgiveness and of reconciliation is one we must aspire each day to achieve.

In the time ahead as we seek to find solutions to difficulties in our own place and in other places around the world we need to remember the words of Nelson "Madiba" Mandela:

> "No one is born hating another person because of the colour of his skin, or his background, or his religion. People must learn to hate, and if they can learn to hate, they can be taught to love, for love comes more naturally to the human heart than its opposite."

# KARINA TUROK

In 1994 I had the privilege of working as the stills photographer on the Island Picture's documentary *Mandela Son of Africa, Father of a Nation*. One of the many memorable moments was when I walked with our film crew and Madiba into the right wing controlled prison office on Robben Island and met with a huge young officer, not more than 25 years of age, and yet someone in a controlling position of the prison at the time. My heart was pounding with the tension and potential confrontation of the moment. The young prison officer was clearly full of hatred, fear and prejudice meeting Madiba. It made such an impression on me observing how Madiba took total control of the situation, how with a warm engaging handshake and smile he totally disarmed the intimidating officer, and diffused the moment with his charismatic confidence, cutting through the hostile atmosphere with his humanity and unpretentious ability to engage without being affected by the initial aggressive cold reception. He softened the air and everything could proceed smoothly as planned.

# ROY
# ANDERSEN

I was privileged to be the President of the Johannesburg Stock Exchange (JSE) for much of the 1990's, a most momentous decade in South Africa's history. Shortly before the first
democratic general election in April 1994 we decided to invite Nelson Mandela to make a speech on the floor of the JSE to send a
message of confidence to foreign investors. This created consternation amongst some members of the JSE; despite the fact that it
was made clear that the State President and National Party leader
FW de Klerk would also be invited at a later date to make a similar speech.

The media attention was enormous on the day Mr Mandela was
to speak and the floor of the exchange was filled with cameramen
from the international television stations. Because of the pressure
of work at the time, the great man was about an hour late. By the
time I was alerted to his arrival and went to meet his car in the JSE
basement, I was feeling somewhat agitated and was ready to rush

him to the floor. The car stopped and the door was opened by a security guard. Mr Mandela said to me: "Please get in."

I was somewhat taken aback, but I got in and sat down next to him in the back of the car. He thanked me for the notes I had drafted for him, which were designed to encourage the foreign investor. Then he said that, having me and discussed arrangements, he was now ready to make his presentation to the members and the media. Needless to say, his speech was a great success. As we left the floor we were surrounded by the JSE's African staff who spontaneously and emotionally started to sing *Nkosi Sikelel' iAfrica* – the first time I had heard what was to become the core of the new national anthem.

Nelson Mandela's composure was inspiring because, even at the height of the election battle and under the constant pressure of being in the public eye, he showed that there is no sense in putting oneself under unnecessary stress. That personal experience confirmed what I already knew – that Nelson Mandela was a most remarkable leader.

# LOVE

"No one is born hating
another person because of the
color of his skin, or his background, or his religion. People
must learn to hate, and if they
can learn to hate, they can be
taught to love, for love comes
more naturally to the human
heart than its opposite."

NELSON MANDELA

# GARY PLAYER

The word that will always come to mind when I think of Nelson Mandela is "love".

The first time I met Madiba, was about a year after his release in 1991. I went to his office in Shell House in Johannesburg. When I went in and saw him, I was so moved that I went on my knees. I took his foot and said: "Mr Mandela, I have never done something like this, but I feel so much love for you and such admiration for what you have done, that I want to kiss your feet". He helped me up and we spoke for a while. I was amazed and touched when he told me how appreciative he was that I had called for his release in 1961 and then he thanked me that I had been involved with sponsoring and training black golfers. When someone who has endured so much and of his stature first of all remembers what you had done and secondly says things like those to you, thanking you, you remember it forever and it means more than all the accolades in the world.

But what always struck me most was his complete lack of hatred. I asked him on that occasion: "How can you be filled with so much love and no revenge for the white man?" Mandela said: "Gary, revenge is like a green apple. It can look green on the outside, but rotten on the inside. We can not live in the past. We must live for the future and we must build a life for everyone." As we were leaving he said: "Gary, please tell your brother (Ian Player) that I have great admiration for what he is doing for the rhino." He actually knew about my family and sent his regards.

During the years we would meet many times and raise a lot of money together for under-privileged children. One of these events was the Nelson Mandela Invitation Golf tournament, which I hosted at Pecan Wood Golf Club. Madiba arrived by helicopter and I had to go and meet him with a golf cart. As he got out of the helicopter I went over to greet him. Before I could say anything he stretched out his hand and said: "Hallo Gary, do you still remember me?" He was truly humble and did not make any assumptions of his own importance or greatness.

Then there is of course his love for children. We were once at my daughter's restaurant Casa Linga. Madiba who was there, was watching all the children play on the lawns around the restaurant. At some point he called them all over and the children were all over him. They climbed on his lap, spoke to him and hugged him and he loved it. For me, any man that loves children, is a great man.

I have met Madiba so many times and yet every time I do, I am close to tears. Not only because I am always conscious of what he had gone through, but also because I am struck by his incredible lack of revenge and the extent of his love for others. He is truly like the great figures of history, Martin Luther King Jnr, and Mahatma Gandhi, a man who oozes great attributes and will go down as one of the greatest leaders in the world's history. My only sadness is that we did not have him for another 10 years as president. But we were blessed to have him and we must be thankful that we had him for those vital years of our new democracy.

Love and forgiveness are at the core of all religions in the world. And as someone who personifies those two values, I believe that he exemplifies and resembles the works of God. For me he will always be the man of love.

# JOVIAL RANTAO

The glass doors swing open. Through them emerge two figures, important yet humble human beings, hand-in-hand.

The one is probably the world's most recognisable icon and political leader – Nelson Mandela. Holding his hand lovingly in support is his wife of eight years – Graça Machel.

Machel is regal and stunning in her maroon suit and traditional braids. Her face has a special glow that reflects happiness and satisfaction.

Her husband is equally resplendent in his traditional Madiba shirt. The couple have just enjoyed morning tea together in their huge, beautifully decorated dining room and have come through to accept a birthday cake for Mandela from readers.

"Hello," Machel says with a smile as she carefully helps Mandela walk towards our party. Madiba also extends his greetings.

We shake hands and reality hits home – the hero of our generation is getting on.

His eyes remain good, his memory faultless, but his knees have begun to tell the story of a man who was born more than nine decades ago in rural Mvezo, in the Eastern Cape, a man who went on to become an international face for the struggle for freedom.

After his release from prison in 1990, he became an even greater icon for reconciliation, reconstruction and development of nations coming out of trying times.

We are at the Mandela home to wish him a happy birthday. As Mandela and Machel move closer together to pose for a photo, we pop the question: "So what did you get him for his birthday?"

She smiles, looks at him and looks back at us: "It's a secret."

At that moment, Mandela jokingly interjects: "She doesn't even give me a kiss."

"Hau! But you get kisses every day," comes the reply, also with a smile.

As they speak, their eyes meet, and the electricity – billions of megawatts of it – is there.

They are like starry-eyed teenagers. Spurred on by the talk of romance, Machel asks photographer Debbie Yazbek to shoot a frame of them kissing.

She is, however, quite clear on the condition under which the photo is taken: "This is for our private (collection) and not for you guys (for publication)."

A second later, we witness an extraordinary moment. It's one that will be indelible.

Mandela and Machel look at each other. They smile. Their eyes seem to close . . . and they kiss. So quick is the kiss that it isn't captured on camera.

"Please do it again," pleads award-winning photographer Debbie Yazbek. They oblige.

What a beautiful moment it was. So perfect and so romantic. So much love. And it dawns on us that, in addition to Mandela's birthday, the couple are celebrating their eighth wedding anniversary.

Good wishes follow and the couple smile in appreciation.

On July 18, 1998, Mandela and Machel tied the knot after a love affair that is likely to go down as the best-kept secret in South Africa and Mozambique.

The marriage came not too long after Mandela's lifelong friend and neighbour Archbishop Desmond Tutu said the time had come for the former president to get some companionship.

"He needs someone to get him his slippers in the morning," Tutu had said.

Through her marriage to Mandela, Machel rewrote the history books. She became the first woman to be married, at different times, to two heads of state.

But Machel is a leader in her own right. She is known to be fiercely independent and compassionate. She runs her own children's foundation in Maputo and is an ambassador for the United Nations Children's Fund.

She also serves on several boards of trustees.

So influential and powerful is she, that political analysts have not ruled out the possibility of her becoming Mozambique's president one day.

After posing for several pictures, Mandela and Machel apologise that they have to leave to honour yet another appointment, part of a series of events organised to mark his 88th birthday.

Machel also apologises for not being able to offer us tea. In true African tradition, she asks us to stay behind after they leave and have something to drink.

She then asks for Mandela's coat. She wants him to put it on.

Mandela enquires about the weather and is quickly convinced by his wife that he needs to cover his frail body because he is going to spend some time at a private clinic in the company of Albertinah Sisulu, a fellow ANC veteran and widow of his late friend and comrade Walter.

At the clinic he will be meeting up with former United States president Bill Clinton.

Clinton is the only president who during his term in office was as tall as or even slightly taller than Mandela.

The coat is brought in by support staff.

Machel takes it and begins lovingly to help Mandela to put it on. First comes the right hand. Then the left. Then she begins to do up his buttons.

"You won't need the gloves," she tells him.

As he takes her hand and they walk away they are clearly a couple deeply in love.

What a perfect picture that makes.

The one thing that was so striking about Mandela was his humility. He had this amazing ability to make his guests, whomever they may be, feel like they were the great Mandela. He would shower them with praises, choosing his words carefully to build your self-esteem.

His humility also extended to his comrades, most of them in their old age. After one of our meetings, an elderly man, wheelchair bound, was wheeled into his office for a few minutes with Madiba. This was a former freedom fighter, now in his old age, just wanting time with the massively popular and powerful Mandela, even in retirement. Mandela would proceed to shower praises on his comrade, for his bravery in the fight against apartheid. The carefully-chosen words brought a smile to the wrinkled face of the comrade. "This is my hero," he said, with a smile. These are the heroes who brought down apartheid."

A few weeks later, he passed away.

The one amazing talent he had, even in his old age, was his memory. Long after he had met two of my children – Mpho and Tumi – he would enquire, by names, about their welfare. That left me with a feeling, as a proud parent, that my children were special.

# LOVE FOR CHILDREN

"There can be no keener
revelation of a society's soul
than the way in which it
treats its children."

NELSON MANDELA

# ALLYSON NEIDER-HOFFMAN

Noluthando School for the Deaf in Khayelitsha, Cape Town was started in 1988 by Mfesane, a welfare organisation. There were no buildings, no children and no teachers. However, there was a tremendous need for such a school in Khayelitsha and surrounding areas. Many deaf children had nowhere to go for an education. The then Department of Education and Training agreed to support a state subsidised school which basically meant that the salaries of the teachers would be paid. In the beginning it was only a principal. Richard Nieder-Heitmann was appointed as principal and temporary buildings were hired.

As funds were raised from overseas and local donors, a new school was gradually built. The number of pupils increased rapidly. However, it was never officially opened in the first ten years of existence. Every now and again the matter of an official opening would be discussed at a board meeting. In the first years of existence, the decision was always that Mandela would be asked to do the opening when he was released from prison. After his release and subsequently becoming president, Madiba was just too busy.

When the matter of the official opening of Noluthando was broached again at the beginning of 1998, one of our board members, (who had ministered to Madiba on Robben Island) was requested to contact Madiba and ask him to do the honours. As it was also the 10th anniversary of Noluthando it was felt that it would be even more special to have Madiba there. To our great joy he agreed.

Madiba's presence was the highlight of the school, teachers, learners, parents and visitors' existence. As he was led to his chair, Madiba picked up a little deaf girl who was in our pre-school and held her on his lap throughout the ceremony. It was as though the grandfather of Noluthando had arrived to enjoy the day with his grandchildren.

When it was time for his speech Madiba pushed his prepared speech to one side. The main theme was that through education no matter what your circumstances, you can make a better life for yourself. He also spoke about how great it was to spend some time with children. He encouraged businesses to get involved in special education. The kids were star struck. They couldn't get enough of him and all wanted to get close to him. His security spent their time shooing off little ones, but Madiba would just wave his hands and say: "Leave them." The kids, who rely so much on their sight, told him that they knew him because they had seen him on TV! You can imagine more than a hundred kids all signing away and gesturing to him about anything and everything. He just loved it.

We later unveilded a bust of Madiba so his presence will always live on in the school.

A truly momentous occasion never to be forgotten by all who were privileged to attend.

# ANABEL
# VAN NIEKERK

In 1997 my husband was chief engineer for the Hamilton Airship Company. They were building a prototype airship of around 50m long in a hangar at the Waterkloof Airforce Base near the terminal used by government officials and VIPs.

One day Mandela came for an informal visit. We, including my son Adam, then seven years old and my daughter Emmerentia (Emmie), ten years old, all shook his hand as he arrived. He was very interested in what was being built. After about half an hour he was at the point of getting in his car to leave when he asked for his 'special friend' to greet him. It turned out he was talking about our son Adam.

About three weeks later the airship was out on the runway for its first test flight. Mandela dropped in again and as usual was surrounded by the children. My children Emmie and Adam met him again. However, as he was walking away my son came to me and asked me why Mandela asked him his name again as he told him what it was at their previous meeting? Of course he did not realise how many children Mandela met every day.

# EMMERENTIA VAN NIEKERK

I was ten years old when Madiba came to visit. I remember him coming to the hangar and being very smiley and chatty. He greeted us all one by one, shaking everyone's hand. He then took a tour around the airship while one of the men explained to him what was happening. Madiba asked a lot of questions. After his tour he went back to his car and made sure to say goodbye to everyone – even calling Adam his "friend".

On his next visit I just remember Adam being upset that Madiba didn't remember him. We explained to Adam that Mandela had probably met thousands of children since his last visit and that he shouldn't be upset.

When I told the children in my class on Monday that I'd met Mandela they all commented on what an honour it was and some of them even wanted to touch my hand that he'd shaken. One girl commented that she would never wash that hand again. Everyone was very jealous.

# CHRISTIAN ROMMERS-KIRCHEN

My father was a diplomat at the German embassy and we stayed in Pretoria between January 1992 and August 1997.

Shortly after he was inaugurated, Mr Mandela threw a party for all the children of the different embassies. My sister, Anne who was six years old at the time and I, who was eight, were invited.

I remember being picked up in front of the Union Buildings in armored 6-wheeled trucks (for security reasons), to be taken to Mr Mandela's house a few minutes drive away. This was one of the highlights for me, as the trucks were very tank-like and it was my first experience riding in any military vehicle.

Upon arriving at the residence, we were sitting in the groups in which we had arrived, all of us a little uneasy and nervous with all the strangers and security staff. While waiting for all the children to arrive, each of us was given a bag of candy, and a magician was performing tricks. Soon the tension in the room was lifted; replaced with laughter and joy.

During the show, one by one, groups were led outside along a small path to where Mandela was sitting on a chair in the shade of an overhanging balcony. Having seen him on TV and with all the talk of him lately because of his election as the President, I was quite excited to meet him. What struck me was how extraordinarily mundane he seemed, and his genuine smile. As if after meeting hundreds of children that day, he was still delighted to meet a few more.

My sister, somewhat to my embarrassment, walked straight to him and shook his hand, which resulted in a few questioning looks among the grown-ups around Mandela. But he just laughed and shook her hand, and realizing that it was all right, I took the opportunity to thank him for inviting us and for the candy.

The photographer and organizer seemed to have a schedule to stick to, so we were hurried into formation. Unfortunately for me, being rather short, I found myself eclipsed behind my sister and just managed to stick my head to the side and make it into the picture as it was being taken.

Moving along, we found ourselves back in the large room where the magician was still performing. My memory has since faded of what transpired thereafter, but I seem to remember some form of speech held from behind the podium and being chauffeured back to the Union Buildings in military style to our waiting parents.

# CHRISTO BRAND

When I became a prison warden on Robben Island and met Mandela he was already 10 years in jail.

There was one occasion when Winnie Mandela came to Robben Island and she brought a baby with her, that was one of his grandchildren. When she ended up at the visiting booth, she was not allowed to bring the child in, because he wasn't allowed to see children under the age of 16. So the child was kept back and held in the waiting room with somebody else. Mandela had the visit after we switched off the microphones. (It was a no-contact visit). He then asked if he could see the child or just touch the child. We said: "No sorry, we can't do that." Then he really pleaded with us that he wanted to just see the child. So Mr. du Preez, who could understand Xhosa, listened to him in Xhosa. He then said: "Christo, go and fetch the child quickly." I went to the other side and said to Winnie: "Mandela wants to see you again in the box for five minutes." When she went to the box, we said she must just wait.

I then said to the other lady: "I want to keep the child for a while."

So I took the child through the back door, and we called Mandela. Unexpectedly, we put the child in his arms. We told him he must keep quiet about it. We could lose our jobs. And he just said: "Oh!" He held the child, he kissed the child; there were really tears in his eyes at that moment. We then took the child out of his arms and took it back to the lady. Winnie didn't know that he had seen the child and the lady inside didn't know where I had taken the child. Nobody ever knew that Mandela had seen the child. Mandela kept it a secret from everybody, I think. And so we were very pleased.

# CONSTANCE MATHEKGA

When my daughter Azwihangwisi was six years old, she was watching TV. Tata Madiba was celebrating his birthday with kids and then he said: "Children the way I love you, I feel like taking you all and putting you all in the pocket of my jacket." From that day my daughter waited for Tata to come and put her in his pocket.

She is 22 years old now and every time she sees Tata on TV or in a newspaper, she laughs and says: "I'm still waiting for *Khulu* (grandfather) Mandela to put me in his jacket." What a great man!

# GEOFF BRUNDRIT

Around 1996, the International World Commission on the Oceans, led by the President of Portugal Dr. Mario Soares, held a formal open meeting in Cape Town. The host was President Mandela and the meeting was held in the old parliamentary chamber at Parliament. With guests (which included me) assembled and seated around the sides of the chamber, President Mandela and President Soares entered the chamber followed by a large contingent of young school children. The meeting commenced with the singing of the National Anthem led by the school children. The children then turned around to leave the floor of the chamber, only to be stopped by President Mandela. President Mandela, accompanied by a bemused President Soares, then stepped down from the podium onto the floor of the chamber and proceeded to speak to **every single child in turn**. The press photographers and cameramen rushed onto the floor to record this memorable. Only then, did the two Presidents return to the podium for the formal proceedings to commence.

# JACKIE AND SASKIA OPPERMAN

JACKIE: In 1998 we were having lunch with friends in Franschhoek when our host exclaimed: "Mandela has just driven past." We rushed outside and saw that a cavalcade of cars had roared onto the farm opposite. My daughter Saskia, who was six years old at the time, wanted desperately to meet Nelson Mandela. She has always loved Mandela and called him "Dela". We went to the farm and rang the bell to the house, but the caretaker refused us entry. Saskia's face fell, she had gotten so far and yet not at all close to him. I suggested she pick some flowers and maybe we could try again. She rushed around collecting flowers and we rang the bell again. With posy in hand, the security guards let only her in to meet her "Dela".

SASKIA: When I think back to that time I vividly remember staring at the dappled sunlight on the lawn while holding the hand of the bodyguard who was leading me to the outside table. As a young child I didn't have an in depth or experienced understanding of what Madiba spent his life achieving for our country, what I did know was that I loved him. Finally, I looked up at the smiling face of my hero. I have never since experienced such an equal feeling of happiness and awe. Madiba offered me food from his table and he chatted to me, while I was sitting on his lap. He asked me what I wanted to be when I grow up and I wanted to impress him, so I said 'a doctor'. He smiled and said: "Wonderful, you will heal me when I am old."

JACKIE: When Saskia returned thirty minutes later, clutching a nectarine Mandela had given her, she sparkled. As the cars left, we rushed out again. Mandela lowered his darkened window and waved his large hand. I looked into his eyes and saw his crinkly-eyed gentleness, compassion and humour. It was a moment that is indelibly stamped in my memory. It was as though we said: "Namaste!" to each other.

SASKIA: I grew up in a South Africa where the name Nelson Mandela resounded with ideas of hope, freedom, peace, forgiveness and love. From my earliest memories, Madiba was a symbol, a presence that watched over us all. In my young mind I associated this man, Tata, as everyone's father and closer to a Divine being than anything else. So the excitement, fear and shock when, just by chance, I was blessed with the opportunity to meet my hero, will stay with me forever. And now we mourn the loss of this great man. While I did not follow the path of medicine and moved into Fine Arts, I know he will always inspire me, and I will always love him.

# JENNI SKIBBE

It was either 1995 or 1996 and I was teaching grade 7 at Good Hope Seminary Junior School in Vredehoek, Cape Town. I had decided to take the class down to the Company Gardens to discuss the architecture of the various buildings along Government Ave. All the learners were scattered around the gardens and some were sitting at the gates of Tuynhuis. I was walking from group to group when I noticed Madiba walking in the gardens of Tuynhuis. He spotted us and then just strolled over to the learners at the gate! In his slow measured way he asked them through the gates what they were doing. They replied that they were sketching the various kinds of architecture of the buildings in the Company Gardens. I was standing behind the learners.

And Mabida responded: "That is good. Remember a good education is the best gift you can give yourself."

He then looked at me and said: " Well done, teacher!"

And then he carried on with his walk.

So many people have commented on the aura of Madiba and it truly was so tangible that day.

# MPHO RANTAO

At the age of four, my brother Tumi and I met a world famous icon for the very first time. Dressed in a green and blue two-piece outfit with my loose dreadlocks, I walked with my parents into the office of the Nelson Mandela Foundation, full of wonder as to why we had to dress up for what did not look like a formal lunch. We reached reception and were greeted by the radiant, legendary Yvonne Chaka Chaka (who looked like my mother's twin), who in turn gave us her award-winning smile, before conversing with my parents for what seemed like an hour. After the introductions were made, we were lead down a bright hallway into an office (or maybe it was a sunroom) and from the doorway I became captivated at the sight of the old man seated on a large, cream high back chair, dressed in a shiny batik shirt and wearing a smile that literally lit up the room.

To me this man looked like God, because he was so happy that even his wrinkles were smiling. My father and Yvonne lead the way towards the old man whose arms were wide open. The only way I could react was to challenge his large smile with my very miniature gap-toothed smile, which went from ear to ear. Tumi on the other hand had a different reaction, as though he was about to cry as we approached the cream sofa. When my father introduced one by one, the old man waved us over, placed me on his lap and spoke (his voice kept making me laugh). He asked who I was and I replied "Mpho!" with such eagerness, that he gave a hearty laugh, before telling me that he was Nelson Mandela. I couldn't stop smiling and felt blown away, but then again I was four, I could have had any emotion flowing though my body. From that point on we entered into a fun conversation which involved my hands showing my age, and telling Mr Mandela how much I loved my family

and friends.

That first meeting in Houghton was just the beginning of many meetings and memories. I last visited Nelson Mandela when I was eleven with my brother. We left during school and were accompanied by our school's counsellor. On that day I felt very proud to be wearing my brown and orange Leicester Road Primary uniform, but I was mostly proud to smile in a photo with Mr Mandela in what I thought was the best photo ever taken.

# NICOLE DEANE

My father, Brian Deane, who is a British ex-pat does not easily show emotion, but on the 11th of February 1990 when Nelson Mandela was released, I found him sitting at the dining table, weeping. When I quizzed him on what was wrong, he simply said: "Nicky, today a great thing has happened." Although I didn't understand it at the time, this was the beginning of my "relationship" with Mandela as my father became determined that somehow we should meet him some day.

Two years later when I was 12 years old my brother and I were called to the principal's office one morning. My dad was there and he announced proudly: "Today, we are going to meet the Prez!!"

My father used to work for a company that sold telephone systems and Johannesburg Central was 'his' area. In January 1995 he called on Shell House as a prospective buyer for the systems. While he was there he mentioned to Madiba's secretary, that his children would love to meet Madiba. Her reply was: "You do know that the President is a very busy man!"

However, eleven months later she phoned my dad and said: "The President has a fifteen minute gap," and told Dad that if he could bring us to Shell House at the specific time, we would be able to meet with Madiba.

So we excitedly made our way from school to Shell House, and waited in the reception corridor for Madiba to make his way through to his office. After a long wait, Madiba arrived in a very trendy looking tracksuit and greeted us all with handshakes and his famous warm smile. He then sat and spoke with us for about fifteen or twenty minutes. He asked lots of questions about us and about our family life. Madiba then noticed that I was wearing my school prefect's badge. He said: "Wow! I see you are a prefect. You are even greater than I am."

I believe that the time spent and the interest shown in both my brother and I, was indicative of his commitment to the children of South Africa.

We were allowed to take a photograph and before long "the Prez", had disappeared on his way again, and we stood in awe at what an incredible privilege it was to be in his presence. We were all just so struck by his warmth and humility. To this day when I think back, I still get goose bumps!

# OSSIE
# GIBSON

The visit by Palestinian Liberation Organisa-
tion leader Yasser Arafat took Tuynhuys a bit by surprise. Mandela
gave Arafat the usual tour of the garden area adjoining Tuynhuys,
with the press (which included me) in tow. As they passed the
fence at the bridge between Tuynhuys and the Gardens, the President noted a group of about thirty schoolchildren who had run
over to the fence when they spotted him, whispering "Mandela,
Mandela". They were determined to have a closer look at the big
man.

"Ah," Mandela said, as they neared the line of little faces peer-
ing through the fence, "thank you for coming to visit us!" The
group of dignitaries waited while he linked arms with a bemused
looking Palestinian Liberation Leader and they went closer to the
kids.

"This is Uncle Yasser," he informed the grade 2's. "He is an engineer and a great leader in his youth even at school. And do you

know even way before that, when he was your age, he always did his homework." He paused slightly: "I hope you do your homework?" Through the bars, thirty or so eager heads could be seen nodding up at him. Yes, they did.

"Good" he said, "then you will also be a big leader, like him."

# RORY STEYN

As part of President Mandela's personal protection team, I witnessed many incidents during my four-year stint that quite often stirred the emotions. However, one in particular stands out in my memory. It involved a state visit by the then President of Ghana, Mr. Jerry Rawlings, in around 1997.

Since parliament was not in session, the ceremony took place at the foot of the Union Buildings in Pretoria.

A state arrival is a highly formal ceremony with strict protocol.

A red carpet covers the driveway in front of the steps leading up to the Office of the President. There is a full military Guard of Honour in front of the red carpet, complete with military band. A 21-gun salute is fired by a battery of four cannon from the nearby Voortrekkerhoogte to welcome the visiting head of state and there is the inevitable press platform behind the Guard of Honour, directly opposite the steps at the foot of which the president would greet his guests. It was there that President Mandela awaited the arrival of President Rawlings.

As was the practice, his motorcade was escorted by a triangular configuration of military policemen dressed up in their finest, trying very hard not to fall off their motorcycles as they could only drive about 15 km/h. We, the security personel, were discreetly placed out of sight.

The door to President Rawlings' vehicle was opened by an *aide-du-camp* dressed in full military uniform wearing white gloves. The President stepped up onto the steps of the Union Buildings, while the motorcade pulled away and he stood shoulder-to-shoulder with President Mandela facing the Guard of Honour. The national anthems of Ghana and South Africa were played, the 21-gun salute fired and then President Rawlings inspected the Guard of Honor, while President Mandela waited for him to return to the steps. Throughout the proceedings, I was positioned on a small ledge behind a pillar,

Once this was all finished, the Chief of Protocol at the time, the late John Reinders, appeared and asked the two heads of state to accompany him into the President's Office for tea and some *tête-à-tête*. Ready to move from my concealed spot behind the pillar, next to a pot plant, I was very surprised to hear Madiba say to John Reinders: "Eh John, roep daardie kind!" (Eh John, call that child!) He pointed across the driveway to a spot next to the press stand. John looked up at me, I shrugged my shoulders and he said surprised: "Excuse me, Mr. President?"

Madiba pointed again and said to John: "Call that child!"

And so in the middle of a state visit, in front of the full glare of the world's media, Madiba asked his Chief of Protocol to call a child to him.

John dutifully went down the steps, across the red carpet, wound his way through an equally confused-looking detachment of soldiers in the Guard of Honour and called the child indicated by Madiba. The Afrikaans-speaking, eleven year-old boy, dressed in his full school uniform, was standing next to the press stand. Slightly bewildered, he followed John Reinders through the Guard of Honour, across the red carpet and up onto the steps. We were all transfixed by what we saw.

Madiba bent down and asked the child his name. Then to everyone's amazement, Madiba turned to his guest and said to the child: "And this is President Rawlings of Ghana!"

The little boy tentatively extended his hand and to his credit President Rawlings, a former Ghanaian Air Force pilot, who is a very impressive, regal man, bent down, shook hands with the child and rubbed his head.

The introductions now complete, Madiba told the boy he could return from whence he came and was now ready to go upstairs to his office with his guest.

I have to confess that I was swallowing pretty hard. There were so many things that this incident was saying to me. It was not just the powerful symbolism of a black president calling a little white boy to greet his guest who was another black president. It also spoke to me of the incredible ability Madiba had to seize upon the little things in life, the things that mere mortals so often ignore or neglect. It was so typical of the Madiba that I had come to revere and to whom my loyalty extended to a commitment to protect with my own life.

Take it from me: Madiba was an extremely busy president. Yet, despite his schedule, he found the time to introduce a child (that he did not know was going to be there) to his guest, whilst totally ignoring the formality of the occasion or the presence of the world's media.

I really cannot think of another leader who would have got away with this and most other leaders would have done it for the purposes of exposure and scoring political points. Madiba never did things for those reasons.

# SHANTI ABOOBAKER

"I can't do it," I whispered to the president, Nelson Mandela, but the elderly statesman insisted on holding my hand. I was an ardent monarchist at the time, to my parents' horror, and was so excited to meet Queen Elizabeth II, but when that moment came, the cameras, the journalists and the dour queen, I became the anxious nine-year-old I really was.

But still holding my hand and nudging me forward Mandela did as he had many times, he encouraged me to be brave and to rise to the occasion – even a small one, such as handing a posy of flowers to the queen of England.

This was the second time I had met Mandela, but this occasion I remember more clearly.

I grew up near Athlone, the eldest child of activists. My room was adorned with posters from the Congress Movement, including a yellow Rivonia Trial poster with photos of released prisoners, including Andrew Mlangeni, Walter Sisulu, Raymond Mhlaba and Elias Motsoaledi.

I learned to sing *Nkosi Sikelel' iAfrika* with a raised fist, a fear of police dogs and stories about Cape Town's famous purple rain protests and the United Democratic Front's launch in Mitchells Plain.

I was almost four years old the first time I met Mandela.

It was May 1990, and the future head of state, not that we knew this for certain at the time, had been free, released after 27 years in jail, for only a few months. I was visiting my mum who was working for the ANC's office at short notice, for the "talks about the talks" at the Lord Charles Hotel in Somerset West.

Frankly I was probably rather anxious to see her after a few nights of being looked after by my dad – I was a mommy's girl back then. "It was very exciting for a lot of people last week, who came in to meet with the leadership for the first time – all the exiles and internal people," my mum said.

And so it was that I sat in a booth at the Lord Charles restaurant on the laps of Madiba, Grandpa Walter Sisulu and SACP veteran Joe Slovo. My mum recalls that Uncle Reg September was part of the ANC's delegation as well – funny they should both pass on in the same short space of time. I imagine wherever they are now, they are all together, having a good old reunion of friends and comrades.

Fast forward to 1995.

Somehow – because even now the details are hazy – it came to be that one Tuesday night over supper my parents mentioned, very by the way, that I wouldn't go to school the next day but would go with my dad to work. My mother had washed my fiercely curly hair earlier, painstakingly combing through the knots, and the dress from my aunt's recent funeral had been ironed.

Queen Elizabeth was in town and I was to hand her a posy of

flowers. It made my heart swoon, but I was instructed I was not to tell a soul. And I was to get into bed.

I had childish and excited insomnia, and my mind raced with optimism. I jumped out of bed the next morning, and my mother tied my hair into a tight, long ponytail, with long curls. I wore the modest dress from the funeral and sat on the back seat as we drove to Parliament, and my dad said very few words.

The visit, above all, was not to go to my head. First port of call was the Presidency, where my dad got on with some work, and I spent some time probably scribbling some thoughts, and drawing some pictures, until someone from Mandela's office came to collect me.

I was a sensitive and intense nine-year-old, keen and eager to meet the Queen and aware that perhaps I might meet the President.

Then it happened. I was taken to meet the President. My ouma's lessons to be a good girl kicked in.

I politely said good morning, and he warmly invited me to sit on his lap, happily chatting away: how are you, what standard are you in, what subjects interest you, and so forth.

And then the words that put me at such ease: "You remind me so much of my grandaughter, Rochelle." President Mandela signed documents, opened letters, until he had to meet the Queen.

The moment was almost upon us.

Standing in the foyer to the steps of Tuynhuys overlooking the Company's Garden, I stood aside as the regal President and the rather dumpy Queen, wearing the dour blue dress, made their entrance. I was lost for words, stunned – and an absolute bundle of nerves, which, if you know me, is generally impossible. Mandela gently took my hand and, all protocols observed, placed me where I was meant to stand. He was so old-hand about it, even though he'd only been doing it for about a year by then. All cameras at the ready I experienced my second bout of stage fright.

My mouth went dry; I'm certain the hand Mandela was holding was cold and sweating. I tried to whisper to him that no, I wasn't ready, I shouldn't, I can't do this. But off he went, nudged me to my place.

I'd been primed to practise my words. "Good morning, Your Majesty. I'd like to present to you on behalf of South Africa this posy of flowers." The queen was way too eager. Before I could say anything, she interjected: "Are these for me? Why, thank you."

And that was it.

I may have been the happiest girl in the world. My dad popped out of nowhere, handed me a sandwich and apple juice, and spent the rest of the afternoon working. We drove back home to Crawford that evening. The Queen was relegated to a distant afterthought for ever more; I was never really a monarchist after she prematurely took her posy!

And Mandela undoubtedly stole the show.

Much as my parents protested, I couldn't help but tell my best friends at school the next morning.

# SHIRLEY NAIDOO

Madiba's love for children is well known, but it was truly exceptional. During one of his stays in Cape Town, a little girl of about six or seven years old arrived out of nowhere at the gate and said she really wanted to meet Nelson Mandela. The police, knowing how Madiba loves children, broke the rules and let her in.

As Mandela's housekeeper I received her. Madiba was having lunch, so I warned the little girl that he might be too busy and suggested we have some tea in the kitchen. She was fine with that, but said she would like to wait for him. So I went to Madiba and said: "Tata, there is a little girl in the kitchen. We do not know her, but she really wants to meet you." He immediately said: "Bring her here!" I took her to the dining room, where she sat with him and they talked and talked. I heard her telling him that she wanted to be just like him, which he enjoyed very much. He was so sweet and kind with her and when he finally sent her on her way she was delighted. What a day the little girl had.

# ROBYN
# VON GESAY

In the year preceding Mandela's inauguration and for a few thereafter I was both a freelance journalist and a stringer, based in Pretoria, for the Reuters news agency.

It was a golden time in terms of access to him: Mandela would stroll into a press conference at the Union Buildings and chat to journalists as he made his way to his seat. He enquired of me as to whether I had children and when on hearing I had two young daughters, encouraged me to bring them to Sunday lunch with his family. I never did take Kerri and Alexa (his time with his family was so precious and rare), but they would meet him, unexpectedly, a few years later in Cape Town harbour . . .

I was present at many functions and press conferences with him. What always struck me was how much he loved being in the presence of children. He would walk up to them, be it at an Afrikaans primary school in Pretoria or a delegation of kids to his office at the Union Buildings and he would say, in that inimitable way of his: "Helllllooo. My name is Nelson Mandela. And what is yours?" He never made anyone think that he assumed they knew who he was.

And he could never be in the presence of children without asking them to join him in singing *Twinkle Twinkle little Star* – and how his eyes would twinkle with delight! A few years later, when my family and I had moved to Cape Town, I was entertaining my daughters and the children of a dear friend and ex-Pretoria News colleague, Ann Donald (we both started our careers there – she would go on become editor of Fair Lady and then to open Kalk Bay Books and now is very involved in the Franschhoek Literary Festival).

I took mine, Kerri and Alexa and Ann's – Andrea and Ryan – to see the iconic cruise liner Queen Elizabeth II which had docked in Cape Town. While there my eye caught some cars which I recognized from my days in Pretoria with Reuters: I was convinced they belonged to the VIP presidential protection unit. "President Mandela is on the ship – we are not moving from here," I told the children. And sure enough, a while later he and Graca strolled down the gangplank. As soon as he saw the children he made a point of coming across to greet them and – of course – to ask them what their favourite song was before launching into *Twinkle Twinkle Little Star*. How I wished I had my camera that day.

One occasion that really resonated with me as I watched Madiba's funeral, is when, in late 1994, he strolled over to chat to us journalists and photographers on the lawn at Mahlamba Ndlopfu, the official Presidential residence in Pretoria. It has a magnificent view to the north of Pretoria, stretching to hazy hills and beyond. It was, if I remember correctly, the day he announced the new

SANDF generals' line-up. I was standing near a coral tree which must have had many a president stand in its shade beneath its brilliantly bright flowers. President Mandela strolled over and started to chat to us in his easy manner. I asked him what his wish would be to do on New Year and he replied that for him, the most favourite thing in the world was to walk in peace in the hills of Qunu. As I watched him being finally laid to rest on that koppie in Qunu that moment came back to me and I thought: *finally, he is there.*

# NOT TAKING HIMSELF TOO SERIOUSLY

"I must step down
while there are one or two
people who admire me."

NELSON MANDELA

# JOHNNY CLEGG

My greatest moment was at a show in Frankfurt in 1997 during a joint Africa-Germany NGO symposium. I ended my performance with *Asimbonanga*. As we began the final chorus, the crowd roared and I was puzzled because it was a strange moment for them to acknowledge the song.

Then out of the corner of my eye I saw a figure behind me. It was Nelson Mandela! He had walked on and was doing his special Madiba move to the music. He stood there beaming and at the end of the song he said: "Music makes me at peace with the world . . . and at peace with myself . . . but I don't see anyone moving out there." He told me to start the song again. We sang another chorus and left the stage together. It was the pinnacle of my career.

# ZAPIRO (JONATHAN SHIPIRO)

In 1999 when Madiba stepped down as President, I was lucky enough to be at his final adress in Parliament as well as the garden party afterwards at Fernwood Estate. We had just made the first life-size puppet of Madiba for the satirical show *ZA News*. I had this idea for Madiba to meet his puppet, so I took it along with me. I had to get it sideways through the metal detector, which looked rather undignified and evoked a few tut-tuts from some people dressed in their finery. However, as soon as I had him on my arm and was imitating Madiba's voice, it was unbelievable how people flocked to it and engaged with it as if it were Madiba himself. I then asked Frene Ginwala, who was Speaker at the time, if there would be an opportunity for me to introduce the puppet to Madiba. At first she was a bit hesitant, but then said I could do it at the end of the event. So I waited with "Madiba" hidden under the table between my knees. After lunch Madiba was getting up to go, so I knew I had to grab the opportunity. I pushed my way to where he was but, not understanding what this was all about, his bodyguards were not impressed. One of them was called "Tall" and for good reason. He tried to block my path, but I ducked past him and approached Madiba with the puppet. He of course had no idea it was about to happen. I stuck the puppet's hand out and Madiba said: "Ah, I believe I have met this gentleman before." It cracked up everyone around us. He then engaged with me for a while, asking how I was, etc. He was so taken with the puppet and so undefensive and ready to make a quick joke at his own expense. For me it showed again how he never took himself too seriously and was willing to laugh at himself. This is a characteristic which I think is so important for leaders to have.

# MELANIE VERWOERD

During a visit to Ireland, Madiba was boarded first for his connecting flight between London and Dublin. Usually VIP's are boarded last and this was clearly a mistake. As was the practise Madiba was seated in Row 1. As passengers filed on everyone wanted to say hello. Zelda la Grange encouraged Madiba to hide behind a newspaper, but he just said: "Why? I enjoy greeting all the people." Finally there was a lull as they waited for one last passenger. He finally arrived and rushed past Mandela. Two rows later, he stopped, and reversed to where Mandela was sitting. In a stong Irish accent he said: "Oi! You're Nelson Mandela, right?" Mandela looked up at him, very seriously. "No, no,"he said. "Many people mistake me for that famous fellow."

# SHIRLEY NAIDOO

Madiba's house in Cape Town, where I was employed as housekeeper, was located in Bishopscourt. It is not the type of neighbourhood where people stare at celebrities or just knock on your door. One day it was extremely hot. Around half past four in the afternoon, Madiba went outside, with his sun hat on and sat at the big front gate, chatting with the security. We were a bit concerned since he was clearly visible from the road. But we need not have worried. Even though he could clearly be seen, everyone – including the domestic workers walking past to catch public transport – just went past. I don't know if they were scared, but I think they just did not expect him. Maybe they did not recognise him, but he was wearing his usual Madiba shirt and in typically Madiba-fashion, waving at them. It was really funny to watch and he was highly amused.

# ORDINARINESS

"I was not a messiah, but an
ordinary man who had
become a leader because of
extraordinary circumstances."

"I do not want to be presented
as some deity. I would like to
be remembered as an
ordinary human being with
virtues and vices."

NELSON MANDELA

# AMANDA CROMHOUT

In 2001, I was general manager for British Airways in South Africa.

We wanted to give Madiba a Premium Card for our Executive Club. These cards are very exclusive (there are probably no more than ten holders in the whole of South Africa) and are by invitation only. I only gave one in my two and a half years as general manager and it was to Madiba.

We arranged to have the card and letter from our chairman, Lord Marshall, hand delivered to Madiba, by myself when he had boarded a flight from Johannesburg to London. On the night I introduced myself and explained about this Premium Card being a gift from our Chairman, etc. Madiba listened politely, took the card, but didn't read it or look at it. He just handed it to his personal assistant, Zelda la Grange, who was accompanying him. He wasn't rude, but not terribly interested in the pomp and ceremony of the Premium Card. Instead he turned to me and said: "But what about

**you**?" He proceeded to engage with me and ask me all kinds of questions, showing genuine interest in me. I felt so touched by this magnificent man.

I didn't spend too long with him, as I didn't want to waste his time, or impose before his flight. I said my goodbyes and he stood up towering over me. It was impossible not to be bowled over by his physical grandeur and amazing presence. I glanced downwards and saw a few holes in his socks!! (He had taken his shoes off for the flight). So my fondest memories are of the magical interest he took in me as a person and the rather charming holes in his socks!

I hope this story won't be embarrassing or disrespectful to him, as it certainly isn't written with that intention!

# ANDREW MELDRUM

It was a Saturday afternoon and I was 15 years old at the time. My dad had decided to take me to Grand Central Airport to have a look at the planes. As we were about to leave, a small passenger plane came in to land and we waited to see the passengers disembark.

To our surprise it turned out to be an ANC delegation and Mr Mandela was amongst the group. The airport was not busy and we were the only spectators there that day.

To be honest it was a slightly scary moment because, although my parents had always been against the apartheid government, Mr Mandela had at that time only been released from prison for around two and a half years and many conservative whites were still referring to him as a terrorist. We weren't sure how the delegation was going to react to the two white guys standing on the edge of the tarmac.

Anyway, our fears were obviously unfounded as Mr. Mandala

simply smiled broadly and waved to us as he walked across the tarmac. We suddenly felt very privileged.

We watched as the delegation left the airport and followed Mr Mandela's car for a little while as we were heading in the same direction. He was being chauffeur driven in his red Mercedes and sat very calmly in the back reading the day's newspaper.

Interestingly there was no police escort or blue light brigade and it all seemed very low key. It was strange to think that we were sitting in traffic next to Nelson Mandela's car in the middle of Midrand and no one else knew he was there.

On the second occasion, it must have been during 1995 or 1996, I was working at CNA Sandton City as a "casual staff member". I was a student and worked evenings and weekends for a while. One evening I was sitting at the information counter with a couple of my work colleagues. All of a sudden the store was completely swamped with people, so much so that the manager had to tell the supervisors to close the shop's doors as we couldn't cope with the amount of people trying to get into the shop. This, despite the fact that it is one of the biggest shops in South Africa.

I didn't know what all the commotion was all about initially, but soon found out that President Mandela was in the store buying stationary – of all things! I don't know how long he had been in the shopping center, but evidently as he was walking through the center he had been spotted and attracted a huge crowd, who then followed him into the CNA!

The stationary department was on the other side of the shop to where the information counter was. So I had to wade through the crowd to the other side of the store until I could see President Mandela. At that point it looked as though it would be impossible to meet him, as he was surrounded by six or so bodyguards who looked like the bodyguards you see in American movies complete with black suits and earpieces with wires coiling down their necks. Pretty intimidating!

Since seeing Mr Mandela at the airport I had become a bit of a devotee and still being an over confident teenager I must have been pretty determined to greet him. I don't think I would be so bold now.

It was almost rude the way I barged my way towards him, but I was determined. Anyway, I managed to get close to him, but then his security held me back. Just as I thought it was never going to happen, I caught his eye and he told his security guards to let me through. And then I shook hands with Nelson Mandela! Unfortunately I was so awestruck that I can't to this day remember what I said to him. I hope I said something along the lines of "it is an honour to meet you, Sir", but I honestly don't remember. I think he said that it was very nice to meet me.

After that, the store manager served Mr Mandela personally, giving him his change and everything, obviously without asking Mr Mandela to queue up at a till and Madiba then left the shop taking the crowd with him.

The shop staff was buzzing for the rest of the evening and I was on an absolute high for the rest of the week. I felt a little bit silly afterwards as though I had behaved like a child falling over himself to get a cricket player's autograph at Wanderers, but I will never regret doing what I did. My parents joked that I was lucky that the bodyguards didn't tackle me to the ground.

I suppose Nelson Mandela shopping for stationary is similar to the way President Obama went to order a burger from his favourite take-away early on in his presidency. A humble thing to do and I think it showed that early on in Mr Mandela's presidency, he had no idea how famous he had become. He literally brought the shopping center to a standstill simply by shopping for stationary.

A lot of famous celebrities shop at Sandton City, especially in the evenings when they are staying at one of the fancy hotels nearby. While I worked at CNA we saw a number of rock stars and people like Richard Branson, but not one of them attracted much of a crowd, let alone filling the shop to bursting capacity as Mr Mandela had done.

As a white male who just caught the tail end of the Apartheid regime, I was born in 1977 and can still remember seeing apartheid discrimination with the "Whites Only" signs and separate queues during the 80s and early 90's as well as the propaganda that the ANC were a terrorist organization with Mr Mandela being the biggest terrorist of all. Meeting Mr Mandela had a very profound effect on me. On both occasions he came across as being so humble, genuinely kind and completely benign. So much so, that it made all the propaganda seem completely ridiculous.

At the same time he had such a huge amount of gravitas and commanded respect without even trying, in a way that is almost amiable. I think it is a very rare quality that he must have developed while having to deal with the hardships he experienced during the apartheid years.

So at a time when many of my friends, teachers and parents of friends were skeptical about the future of South Africa during the early to mid 90's, I was always positive about the future. For me, that had a lot to do with witnessing, however briefly, at first hand how kind and forgiving our President was during that time.

# BARBARA HELEN MYBURGH

As someone in my fifties, I have many memories of the old Apartheid government.

The day Mr. Nelson Mandela came into my life was more than meeting the President of South Africa. He left an impression on me that left me feeling so special, but also shocked to this day.

I worked in the drawing office of Map Studio in Wynburg, in the Northern Suburbs of Johannesburg.

It was a sunny day as I worked in an open plan office on the first floor that overlooked the car park. Suddenly someone brought to our attention that there was something strange going on outside. We looked out the window and saw that there were all these big black cars with men of all races who were armed and that the car park had been closed to the public.

One of my colleagues went downstairs to find out what was going on and there, to his surprise, he saw Mr Mandela in the sales office. It turned out that Mr Mandela had come to buy a map for his office in Houghton. Just imagine the shock and disbelief of everyone as we could not believe that presidents shop for themselves and especially not in an area which was not that safe. (We were in an area well known for hijackings). Not one of us had **ever** even seen a member of the old government in public.

Everyone was arguing over who was telling the tallest story and if it was really him. Most people felt that we could not go down to see if it was really him, since the security was there and would stop us. I decided to go and have a look and to my relief everyone followed behind me. Now you must know at this point this is the most daring thing I had ever done.

The funny part was that the stairs had a landing between the first floor and the ground floor. In order to see downstairs, we had to stand on the landing, turn our backs to him, bend down and look between our legs, or sit, or lie on the floor. Can you imagine what those big men with guns and suits must have thought of us?

However, they were gentlemen and came up to us, but we started to run away in fear. Then one of them said we could come back and greet Madiba after he was done with his business. We were told where to stand and for the first time in my life, I did not question anything. I just ran down and stood where I was told. **everyone** joined me and waited with so much excitement. Our manager shouted at us to get back to work, but we all ignored him.

When Mr Mandela was finished and came out of the office he looked surprised and shocked to see all the staff crammed in a stairway to see him. Wow! He shook my hand and everyone else's and spoke to us all. He did not even seem rushed. He took his time talking and laughing with us and thanked us for coming to see him.

Afterwards he took the sales manager to his house in Hough-ton to see if the map would fit where he wanted it to hang. She went with him in his car. Not even a separate car! We could not stop talking about it all for months. This was the first time in our lives that a man of his position spoke to ordinary people, like us.

To tell you how much no one really believed that a president would do his own shopping; the receptionist and manager of Map Studio were contacted by his security so they could clear the sales office in advance. However, she put the phone down on the secu-rity three times before passing it to a manager who nearly also hung up.

This was more than meeting a great man; it was so much more. Enough for me who is no writer to try to tell you how excited, hum-bled and shocked we were that he would do this.

I will never forget it. It still gives me goose bumps to this day.

# JAMES WHYLE

When Nelson Mandela was freed and walked proudly out of the Victor Verster prison I watched with my wife and children and friends and the rest of the world in the sitting room of our house in Johannesburg.

Some years later I stepped out the back gate and bumped into my friend John Maytham. John, who is now a broadcaster, was dropping his son off at the play school next to the Synagogue next door. He had performed with the Aeroplanes in the old days. He did a horse race commentary where the horses had names like *African Nationalism* and *Naked Racism* and *Logical Positivism* (a rank outsider). The Racist Regime was still in full swing then and the audience would roar with laughter when *Total Anarchy* took the race by a length.

John and I chatted for a bit and then he said:

"There's Nelson Mandela."

I looked up and there he was. He walked out of the playschool with his grandson and two low-key bodyguards. A white mother recognized and greeted him. He chatted to her.

It occurred to me to introduce myself. But the sunny Johannesburg morning was so peaceful. It seemed an unnecessary intrusion. A grandfather was picking up his daughter's child from playschool. Let it be. Mr Mandela smiled and nodded to the woman. After a couple of minutes they parted and he drove off in a black Mercedes. I looked around. A domestic servant was chatting to a friend on the corner. A Hassidic man hurried into the Shul. I could hear my wife calling the children.

# MICHAEL DE HAAST

In 1996, as the General Manager of The Courtyard Hotel in Pretoria, I had the great pleasure of befriending the Kuwaiti ambassador to South Africa, Ambassador Nabeela Al-Mulla. The previous year, she had been instrumental in arranging Nelson Mandela's visit to Kuwait and had herself travelled along with the entourage. She told the most amazing stories of how President Mandela interacted with the ordinary folk in and around the palace he was staying at – breaking all of the protocols which so stringently accompany a state visit of this nature. One such story was of how Madiba woke up early one morning and wandered around the palace talking personally to each of the guards he came across, asking them about their families and experiences. He ended up outside the palace grounds, much to the shock and horror of the security teams which were frantically searching for him. He was eventually found, interacting with locals, across the street of the palace grounds. This amazing story had a substantial effect on my perception of President Mandela and his obviously deep sense of humanity and humility. It brought about within me an even deeper desire than before to meet this inspirational world leader.

# NANCY RICHARDS

Soon after Mandela's release from prison, he addressed the Cape Town Press Club. The event took place at the Kenilworth Racecourse, which seemed a bit incongruous.

I remember being transfixed as he spoke, as if collectively we all hung on every word. But, afterwards no one dared to ask him a question. Eventually there may have been one or two nervous attempts, but it's not often you hear the press fall silent.

Later, the formalities over, we all gathered around and he greeted us warmly, shaking hands and smiling. He took my proffered hand, and I remember plucking up the courage to ask the rather lame and banal question that had been playing in my head. It was something to the effect of: "What are you looking forward to most now that you're out of prison?"

"To play with my grandchildren," he replied.

So simple, so honest.

# SHIRLEY NAIDOO

Despite who Madiba was and all the great and famous that surrounded him, it was the little things that seemed to make Madiba happy. As his housekeeper I saw, for example, the pleasure he got from feeding the fish in the pond in front of the house. Then there were Graca and Mandela, the two Egyptian geese, so named because the same pair had been visiting the garden of the house in Cape Town for years. During his visit in 2011 Madiba was very ill, but to his surprise and joy the geese had just had a few babies. While recuperating Madiba sat for hours on his chair in the lounge and watched the geese and their babies through the window as they waddled around the garden. He was totally intrigued by them and would laugh at their antics, saying how happy it made him to watch them.

He never lost the ability to find joy and pleasure in the simple things in life.

# STEVE
# SMITH

Rushing up to us in an excited manner, Dan gushed: "Come and see the big man!" Keith and I had popped in to the restaurant CJ's in Main Road, Rondebosch, principally to have supper, but also to catch up with our old mate from the Eastern Cape, Dan, who was managing the restaurant. It was the mid 90's. At the time, we had not been seated very long, and I honestly wasn't **that** interested in seeing some 300kg guy (I'll never forget – that was the number that lodged in my brain!) who I thought was uncomfortably sitting somewhere in the restaurant. I was sure that an obesely overweight individual didn't want arbitrary people ogling him.

Nevertheless, Dan insisted, so Keith and I quickly gulped a mouthful of cold beer and reluctantly followed him. He led us outside. And there across the road, was the Madiba entourage. I forget how many there were, but perhaps about a dozen people spread out over about 25 metres, trudging slowly on the pavement towards

Claremont. Bodyguards were walking both ahead of, and behind a small cluster of people, in the middle of which was the great Nelson Mandela. I was transfixed, and stood there for several minutes as they slowly made their way past us, and I watched until the darkness of the night enveloped them. Apparently, this was a regular ritual for Madiba, which I found fascinating, because it seemed so open, placing him in a potentially vulnerable situation. With a resigned sigh, and a huge smile on my face, exceedingly chuffed at Dan's insistence that we come see 'The Big Man', we returned to our table inside and proceeded to enjoy our meal.

I'm pretty sure it was more than an hour later, Keith and I still at the restaurant, when suddenly there was another excited 'buzz' filtering though to us where we were seated around the corner towards the back. "He's back!" I heard someone say. I immediately leapt up, and with Keith hot on my heels, we proceeded outside. I'll never forget . . . there was Madiba talking to some of the patrons at the outside tables, shaking hands. They'd obviously strolled up towards Claremont, crossed over the road and were returning on the restaurant side. I was in absolute awe. Here was the icon; the saviour of South Africa; and in my opinion the greatest human being the world has ever seen within arm's length from me! Exactly what was being said I'll never remember, but I do recall hearing an Aussie twang from one of the seated patrons.

Seeing Madiba having contact with ordinary fellows like me, shaking their hands, meant I was certainly going to get in on the act. It was a once-off opportunity. I boldly stepped forward, and at an opportune time thrust out my hand. He turned, looked me in the eye, and . . . We shook hands! What I said, escapes me, but it was probably something inane like "it's pleasure to meet you".

Madiba did the same with Keith, and then a security guard promptly stepped forward and separated Nelson from other eager hands.
Enough was enough. At that, Madiba was quickly surrounded by
broad-shouldered guys and they slowly ushered him back onto the
pavement, homeward bound.

I have relived that evening countless times since then, and the
feeling of shaking hands with Nelson Mandela will live with me
forever.

# SENSE OF HUMOUR

"You sharpen your ideas
by reducing yourself to the
level of the people you are
with and a sense of humour
and a complete relaxation,
even when you're discussing
serious things, does help
to mobilise friends around
you. And I love that."

NELSON MANDELA

# BRUCE FORDYCE

My favourite sports award is the State President's Gold Award for Sport, which I received from President Mandela himself. At the time some retrospective awards were given to has-beens like myself who had not received awards during the National Party government's regime. I was never going to be given an award or any recognition from the Nats after I wore a black armband in the 1981 Comrades marathon as a protest against the race's incorporation into the Republic Day Festival celebrations. However, the wait was truly worth it, and it was the highlight of my sports career to be honoured by our greatest citizen alongside other sporting luminaries like Jody Scheckter and Basil D'Oliveira.

Madiba had a special word for each of us and when we left the stage each of us was a little star-struck. As I walked up to receive my medal and certificate he looked at me, and smiled and said, "Ah, here is our Bruce, the man with more comrades than the ANC!"

# FLAVIA KIRUNDA

I was working for Kellogg Foundation in 2006 and our Regional Director at the time, Bishop Malusi Mpumulwana, organised for the Kellogg team to meet Madiba a few days after his birthday.

We were advised that Graca Machel had suggested that the team visit their home in Houghton for tea.

I didn't sleep a wink the night before the trip. Emotions ran through me like the river Nile, which I happen to know very well as a Ugandan. I remember waking up at 4:00 am and thinking I was late to head to the office.

We arrived at the house and were briefed on protocol and also that Madiba's eyes were deteriorating and therefore no flash photography was allowed. Mrs Machel met us as we entered the house and shook our hands. Madiba was seated and as we walked into the lounge he stood up. The aura that surrounded him and filled the room was a phenomenon. He shook my hand with a strong grip. Emotions gushed through me again. How can a Ugandan girl be so lucky to meet this global icon that so many people only dream about! I was turning 40 the following month and the saying that life starts at 40 made sense at that point.

Although we were briefed on flash photography, I completely forgot that my camera was on flash and I quickly pulled it out so I could capture the icon on my personal camera. To my surprise as well as others in the room, it flashed on Madiba's face. I could have died from the piercing looks I received from my colleagues, but Madiba quickly said to me: "Don't worry. Maybe your flash is the one to fix my eyes." The room broke out in laughter. I was immediately put at ease by Madiba's kind sense of humor.

One special story I remember vividly that he told us on the day was one about pigs and how they love alcohol! As young boys they would drop bits of fabric soaked in alcohol along the pigs path leading to a hollow ditch. The pigs would then follow the smell and eventually fall into the ditch and the boys would spear the pigs and have a good roast in the fields.

I will forever cherish the moments I spent with Tata Madiba. Meeting him with Mrs Machel in their home was very special.

# GEOFF BRUNDRIT

Around 1997 or 1998 there was a special gradu- ation ceremony at the University of Cape Town, to which Nelson Mandela was invited. At this stage it was known that Nelson Mandela and Graca Machel had commenced a relationship. On the day with many important guests assembled on the stage of the Jameson Hall, President Mandela was the last to arrive. He appeared at the side door and walked very slowly and deliberately into the hall and up the steps to take his seat on the stage. He then rose as the first speaker to greet the guests and to set the scene for the occasion. He started in a jocular fashion and teased the audience. "When you saw me coming in, I could sense that you were looking at each other and thinking *Oh he's getting old* and *Oh, he's getting frail*. But I want to tell you that the reason that I came in so slowly, is that I wanted to act in a proper and dignified manner, as befitting my office." He then turned to Archbishop Tutu and said: "Desmond here has told me off about many things, including my relationship with my friend, Graca. He said that I'm not setting a good example to the youth. Perhaps my dignified entry will help reassure him."

# PIE-PACIFIQUE

Picture a young Rwandan refugee in Durban, South Africa, with no family or close friends and only a few weeks before his 21st birthday. He wakes up early to his routine: switch on talk radio (SAfm to be precise) to listen to current affairs and learn English, walk to the bathroom, wash face with cold water, walk to kitchen to make sorghum porridge, and a few minutes later, finish dressing by tucking his worn out black jeans in his ageless heavy leather boots. He counts coins, sets aside the taxi fare in his pockets and separates the sum of seven rand he must pay to hire the black polyester jacket that allows him to claim a spot along the road or in a parking lot as a parking attendant.

Today, his spot will be outside the main gates of the University of Natal. The trick there is to stand as far as possible from the gates, because the further motorists leave their cars, the more inclined they are to give a tip to the car guard when they return and find all is well. Almost all of them here are students at the University. Most of them don't tip, and a five rand coin from one of the few who care to show some appreciation is enough for the young refugee to remember their face, the make and colour of their car for a long time. When anyone of them gives him a gift of conversation, he is ecstatically happy, and it is almost always about what happens on the other side of the guarded gates. Increasingly curious and still plotting how to become one of the privileged ones who swipe a card at the turn-style gate, he guards the cars against car thieves and window breakers all day until the sun sets.

Well, that was me in 2001. Now fast forward: we are sometime late January 2006. Two months previously, I was informed that after the long selection process, I was elected as one of the fifteen Mandela Rhodes Scholars for 2006. Today, we have been brought to the Nelson Mandela Foundation offices in Houghton to be introduced to the Patron of the Mandela Rhodes Foundation. We are all waiting for the former president to arrive. Journalists scrambling for the best spot in the house, and cameras are clicking without flashing. A constant thought goes through my head: how on earth did I end up here, me of all people? Overwhelmed, I am struggling to refrain from crying, barely managing to contain the tears. I am wondering what one talks about when you meet Nelson Mandela, and in front of so many people including major news outlets. As I think I should, I take it extremely seriously, and I am really nervous.

I find it hard to believe that my first encounter with Nelson Mandela is only a few minutes away, and that a long-held dream is about to come true. In fact, it was when I was only nine years old that my home teacher in Rwanda instructed me to listen to the radio back in 1990, because 'something important was happening

in the world'. The significant event was the release of Nelson Mandela from prison, which was being broadcast live in several languages just like big football games and the Rwandan president's
speeches. On that day, as I felt Mandela's power vibrating in my
own country, I began to dream about the moment I would meet
and shake hands with him!

Now that it is about to happen, I am so happy but nervous that
I don't know what to do with myself.

I don't notice the time passing. Moments later, Nelson Mandela
himself is sitting in one of the two chairs set in the front of the
room. The other chair on his right side is for each one of us as we
go up and meet the Madiba, one by one. Shaun Johnson, the CEO
of the Mandela Rhodes Foundation calls my name. For a moment
I hesitate as if I didn't hear it. He keeps talking, but I don't get what
else he is saying about me as I stand up and step forward to greet
Mandela and sit in the chair besides him, still wondering what I
am going to say. After the timeless handshake, he speaks first.

"So young man, you are from Rwanda?"

"Yes, Sir!"

He points his right finger at me, slowly moving his hand up and
down.

"Eeh . . . Who is the president of your country?"

"It is Paul Kagame, Sir!"

"Oohhh! It is still that guy?"

At this point, I can't help but laugh, which is not hard, because
he actually laughs first, and everyone in the room follows! The
jovial conversation continues. I have no idea how, but now I feel
so relaxed as if we have already met many times before.

\* \* \*

As a refugee from Rwanda who had to leave my country after the 1994 genocide, meeting Nelson Mandela brought me a whole new dimension in my quest to understand what forgiveness really is and how far it can be stretched. I shook hands with the man who refused to be consumed by resentment, despite all that he endured that could have justified any revengeful behaviour on his part. And yes, he is human . . . deeply human. I now understand and believe that what he has done is the human thing to do, and how he has been is the human way to be. I now understand that the revolution he has started goes beyond forgiveness between different races of South Africa, and extends even far beyond the people of Africa many of whom are still trapped in cycles of war and violence. In a significant way, knowing what the man who shook my hand could overcome has empowered me to fight the only battle worth fighting: the liberation of my soul from fear, greed and resentment.

Thank you Tata Mandela. By being the man you are, you invited me to take a stand on truth, forgiveness and respect for all human beings! I heard the call!

And thank you for a great sense of humour!

# MELANIE
# VERWOERD

In December 2006, I was part of an exclusive lunch with Madiba at the house of the head of the Mandela-Rhodes Foundation, Shaun Johnson. I was sitting at a table adjacent to where Madiba was sitting. At some stage he spotted me and waved me over to come and say hello. He greeted me warmly and asked how I was. I, in turn, asked how he was keeping. "You look really well, Madiba," I said. He sighed heavily. "No, no Melanie," he said, looking very grim-faced, "I am getting very old." "Really?" I responded. "I don't think so." "You see," Madiba said slowly with a twinkle in his eye, "the young women don't like me so much any more." "Well, I still fancy you, Madiba," I joked. "Ja, but you are not so young anymore!" he responded in a flash and we both burst out laughing. Many a true word spoken in jest!

# MICHAEL ATTENBOROUGH

*Michael Attenborough on behalf of his father, Sir Richard Attenborough.*

Shortly after being elected president, Madiba sent my dad a message that he would really like to meet him – *Cry Freedom* being the connection of course.

Madiba asked Dad to let his office know on his next trip to South Africa so they could meet. On my dad's next trip to South Africa with my mother, he duly informed Madiba's office. The only problem was that Madiba was travelling at the time and as it turned out, Madiba was getting back the night before my dad and mom were about to fly back to Britain. My dad ensured the staff that it was no problem and that they could do it at a future opportunity. However, Mandela's office got in touch with Dad to say that when Madiba heard about it, he insisted that he really wanted to see Dad. The problem was that Madiba was arriving only late the previous night and my parents were leaving at the crack of dawn the next day. Still Madiba said that he would really like to see them early in the morning, before they leave, if they were agreeable. Of course my parents agreed.

On the particular morning, they were courteously greeted by a staff member at his residence. She asked them to wait while she informed Madiba they were there. She said that Madiba had expressly asked to be woken so he could say hello. So my parents were standing downstairs as Madiba came down the staircase in a rather spectacular pair of white pajamas and greeted my father and my mother. As he shook my mother's hand he said: "I can definitely tell you, that you are the first white woman that I have ever met in my pajamas!"

Whenever my dad tells this story he doubles up with laughter and my mum duly blushes.

Years later, my dad was interviewed by Michael Parkinson, who asked about a story he had heard, that Nelson Mandela had told my dad that *Cry Freedom* had convinced more white South Africans that Apartheid was wrong than any speech Madiba ever made. To which my dad replied: "Yes, he did say that to me, but we all know of course that Madiba is a terrible liar!"

# NICK
# BEZUIDENHOUT

In August 1996, members of the Islamic vigilante
movement Pagad murdered Rashaad Staggie, a gang leader, in
public and in the presence of members of the South African Police
Service. An aspect of the police's response to the ensuing criticism
was that it had not been aware of the extent of Islamic militancy in
South Africa.

Shortly afterwards, as a journalist for *Beeld* newspaper, I wrote an
article based on a classified police intelligence report about Islamic
extremism and militancy in South Africa that a source had leaked
to me. The intelligence report predated the Staggie murder by
about six months and the purpose of the article was to show that
the police's excuse of not having been aware of the Islamic militancy issue was rather lame.

Members of the police's counter-intelligence unit came to *Beeld*'s
Johannesburg offices in their grey suits and grey shoes with a
search warrant and confiscated my copy of the intelligence report.

They wanted to know who my source was, but I refused to say. So, using a piece of apartheid legislation, they subpoenaed me to appear in court to say who my source was. If I refused to reveal my source, I could be sent to prison until I changed my mind. Obviously the approaching court appearance and possibility of being sent to prison filled me with dread. I could only hope that the political implications of throwing a journalist in jail in the New South Africa would somehow count in my favour.

Two days before I had to appear in court the police informed me, to my great relief, that the subpoena had been withdrawn. I knew that they still didn't know who my source was, so I could only assume that the decision to withdraw the subpoena had been a political one.

My assumption was all but confirmed when, shortly afterwards, I attended a press conference (on an unrelated matter) held by (then President) Nelson Mandela on the front lawn of his house in Houghton, Johannesburg. It was the first time that I had seen him in person. During question-time I asked a question and also stated my name and the newspaper I worked for, as is customary. Mandela looked at me with a twinkle in his eye and said, with mock surprise in his voice: "Oh, I thought you were in prison!"

I will never know whether the decision to let me off the hook and therefore to save me from going to prison was his, but I would like to believe so. And I feel honoured that he took the trouble to recognise me, even if it meant being teased in front of the South African press corps.

# PIETER-DIRK UYS

Now, to get an interview with Nelson Mandela is probably the hardest thing in the world to arrange. Everyone wants to talk to him. He is the most remarkable politician in the world. He has a wisdom and a charisma that promise good copy. He tries to fit all into his schedule, but he is only human, contrary to what many people may think.

When *Funigalore* started, it was the unspoken dream that maybe one day Nelson Mandela would agree to take part. But we had to audition for him. I had to show him my cards.

After the first series it was obvious that what we were doing was being regarded as more than just a comedy turn with a man in drag. The viewing figures had shot up. Everyone was talking about the programme. Politicians started making their interest known. I wrote a letter to the President in September, asking his indulgence. It would be fun, I suggested. An official letter arrived sometime during the next month saying: Thank you but no. There is no time.

By now, however, we had tried other sources. His daughter Zinzi seemed sympathetic and would put in a word. I left a letter for the President at the High Rustenburg health farm when I heard he was due to arrive the day I was leaving. It would be fun, I promised. The memory of our first meeting earlier in the year at the Retreat rally on Valentine's Day was still strong in my mind, and the knowledge that one framed photo on Nelson Mandela's desk was of him and Mrs Bezuidenhout, gave me the feeling that all was not in vain. And so it came to pass that suddenly we were told he would grant us an interview!

We got to Tuynhuis at 7 am to do the make-up. Gail, a Cape-based makeup artist, was with me. The idea of being in the same room as Mandela was nearly too much for her and she was seriously excited. We were welcomed by all, security at the gate, the door, the inner door, the foyer and the passage. They were young and seemed to look forward to the fun. As for me, I had that visit to the dentist feeling, with my toothache in the pit of my gut!

The reception room was full of activity when Mrs Evita Bezuidenhout entered. I was in full costume and make-up. No one seemed to notice.

I went through the half open door to find a private moment just to take a few breaths. It was the Cabinet room. An oblong table bristling with microphones and high-backed chairs, all facing the throne at the top. Was this where all the decisions were made in the old days? I looked out of the window into the gardens of Tuynhuis. Half a dozen gardeners were pottering around. Peace and calm. Table Mountain loomed to the left, Parliament to the right. Our own Versailles. Number 10. White House. Elysee Palace. Kremlin.

I went back into the room. Two chairs stood facing each other like an electric chair reflected in a mirror. Evita Bezuidenhout sat down and was strapped in with mic cables.

Then suddenly the bustle was gone. There was a deep and terrible silence. Probably the most unsettling thing, to suddenly see a film crew ready and waiting. One could hear the adrenalin pop in various stomachs.

I wanted to pee. I wanted to *poep*. I wanted to run. But Evita wanted to see Madiba and so we all sat and waited. He was to come in through a door behind me.

Tick tock tick tock. My eyes scanned the faces of the crew. For each one this was a momentous occasion. No mistakes. No time. No programme.

Then we all heard the familiar nasal tones. He was outside in the passage. The door opened and he walked in. I was watching Gail as she looked at her hero. Tears spurted from her eyes and she hugged herself in an agony of delight. President Mandela was wearing a loose shirt in a black and white design. I was pleased I'd chosen the floral for Evita and not the second choice which was a black and white design. The President and the *Boere tannie* could've looked like matching armchairs!

Mandela went round to each member of the company, shaking hands and welcoming them. I'd been told not to move, because of the mic cable up my dress, but bugger that. When Nelson Mandela turned to me, I half rose. He was twinkling.

"Ah, and there you are, looking so beautiful."

I think I said: "Mr President, we can't go on meeting like this ..."

We embraced. He felt thinner than last time. He sat in his chair and I plopped down in mine. Mercifully the camera didn't show my feet, for they'd gone completely awry. I'd just stopped thinking with anything else but my head. Evita sat there like a ragdoll, feet pointed in, knees apart!

Mandela got his mic clipped onto his shirt. He was smiling broadly at me.

"Thank you for your time," I said. "This is a great honour."

He then said how important he thought the programme was. "Evita says things that people listen to." I immediately knew we were on the same wavelength and started looking forward to the interview.

There has been so much written about this man, so many articles and interviews and stories and legends, and yet to prepare for a chat like this was nearly impossible. Firstly, there was no way that I would make him look bad, not a moment of embarrassment for him, certainly no hint of send-up. He was the President. He was Mandela. He was a hero. In the past it was my joy to break down the false gods. Now it was my duty to support the true leaders. The fact that he was prepared to expose himself to the likes of an Evita, to the whims of a stage comic dressed up as a woman, that in itself was enough of a joke. I didn't need to pull out any washing and hold it up in the sun.

I smiled at my friend in the chair across from me. He nodded and winked. We were off.

"Mr President, everyone in the world wants to spend time with you and here you are with me. I must thank you." A nice opening moment offering him the chance to say: it's a pleasure. Or whatever. He does nothing. He just smiles. Oops. She carries on. "It's a wonderful honour to be back here in Tuynhuis . . ." Again he just smiles and nods. An icy panic shoots through my tummy. Please,

Madiba, don't encourage a monologue! "I look around this room and I see some of the things that I helped create. Mrs Botha and I looked after the curtains here."

Mandela looks startled and peers around at the curtains. Pink and lime green. "Oh yes?" The ice is broken.

"Do you enjoy being in Tuynhuis?" *Mevrou* asks.

He answers slowly. Yes, he enjoys being in Tuynhuis, "because it gives one an opportunity to make a humble contribution towards the national debate that is going on in the country. And yes . . . er . . . it's a wonderful experience." I'm not quite sure what all that means, but Evita sails into mined waters, flags a-flying.

"We were very scared in the old days, as you probably remember. Afrikaners like me were frightened that when black South Africans would take control of South Africa, all the old symbols, the old paintings, the old stinkwood furniture would be removed and we're so happy to see that everything is still here."

He remains in his serious mode. I feel I'm getting Answer 45/b. Change the subject! When in doubt, P W Botha!

"Did you meet President P W Botha in this room?" He did indeed.

"I met him in the room where I am."

"What was the experience like?" Evita asks, echoing the question on a million lips.

"It was an experience, you know, which shook me from top to bottom. Because I had expected that . . . er . . . he would behave in the way in which his image had always been projected . . ." An image I hoped I had contributed to projecting! ". . . that he would lecture to me and pointing a finger . . ." I can't resist Evita pursing her lips and wagging a little finger here. Nelson twinkles. "But it was one of the most pleasant interviews I've had. He welcomed me with a broad smile and he served tea for me and . . . er . . . and it really was a wonderful meeting."

Imagine it: P W Botha, Emperor and White *Induna*, pouring tea into a china cup for the tall black man in a new grey suit brought in from his jail cell to meet his jailer.

"Did you have *koeksisters* with your tea?" Evita asks.

"Why?"

"Because I sent *koeksisters* specially for you that day," she purrs.

He laughs. "Well, on that day they were not there. But *koeksisters*, you see, are my favourite." That's a new one! "In fact, when I reached Johannesburg in 1941, I saw *koeksisters* for the first time." I don't want to interrupt. Evita murmurs a delighted *"Ja?"*

"And at that time I was getting two pounds a month, but I used to reserve ten shillings, so that every weekend I could have *koeksisters!*"

343

"Well," glows the *Moeder* of the *Nasie*. "I shall make a point of sending you *koeksisters* once a month!"

Mandela beams that magical smile. "Oh! Thank you! First class!" He gives the thumbs-up with both hands, sharing his delight with everyone in the room.

Isn't it time for the ten minute signal? Every moment feels like an hour! I page through my mental notes.

"Mr President, I see the beautiful garden here at Tuynhuis. Still exquisite and so special. Do you have a chance to, as in the old days . . . I read in your biography, you wore a straw hat at Pollsmoor and worked in the garden? Do you have a chance to enjoy yourself here?"

A serious expression removes memories of *koeksisters*. "Well, that is one of the things I regret very much. Because in prison I could sit down at the end of the day. And *think!*" He articulates the word as if it means "celebrate". "Do nothing else but *think.* And I was able therefore to see myself in a different light and to be able to correct the mistakes. .. at least to have a plan to correct the mistakes we committed in the course of our work." I wonder how many other interviewers have heard this. To me it sounds fresh and personal. I nearly forget to act. He pauses, but I say nothing. Nor does Evita. "And the other thing that I liked very much was gardening. To create something new. I spent at least two hours a day gardening. I have no time for that now."

"Oh, what a shame," murmurs Evita wondering whatever happened to hard labour in jail.

"I don't even have the time to think!" Mandela repeats. "I have to move from one meeting to the other, and by the time I go back home, either at ten o'clock, sometimes at twelve o'clock and even after, all that I have to do is just go to bed!"

The loneliness of this man affects us all. Is there anyone waiting for him at night to make him some cocoa? Dying to ask him; damned if I can.

"Where is your home, President Mandela? Where do you feel most at home?" Evita has also heard of the stories of the former First Lady's dismay at having to move out of their Pretoria palace, *Libertas.* Mandela moved in and renamed it *Mahlambandlophu.*

"Well, Lower Houghton now is my home." His pronunciation makes it sound like Lower Gauteng! "In fact, I wanted to stay in Lower Houghton and travel every day to Pretoria. But there was solid opposition against this. Even Mr de Klerk told me that he thought it would be risky for me to stay in Lower Houghton, and strenuous too. And he advised that I should stay in Pretoria. When Parliament is here, of course, naturally I must spend most of my time here. And be able to be in contact with Cabinet Ministers, members of Parliament, because that is very important." The President is not a Member of Parliament. "I can't understand how the Head of State could be excused from being a Member of Parliament where the fate of the country is being decided."

"Table Mountain. Has this become a symbol for you through the years?" Evita asks.

The President smiles. "Well, Table Mountain *is die ou Vader van die Moederstad*, and so it has got that symbolic significance for us. I went up Table Mountain in December '47 and I saw Robben Island from there. I never knew that I would be an inhabitant of Robben Island for more than two decades!"

"I remember also when you were at Pollsmoor, you used to come into Cape Town with, was it Luitenant Gregory?"

"Oh yes," he answers forcefully – obviously a strong memory.

"I think I once saw you sitting in the car. I saw the police officer go into a shop. I looked into the car. I saw you. I said to myself: "*O! Liewe aarde, daar is Nelson Mandela!*" I think you were eating an icecream . . . "

"Oh yes!" he remembers, cupping his chin in his hand, twinkling away, being entertained.

"I wanted to open the car door and say: "Mr Mandela, let's run away together! Let me save you!" But I was so scared you would turn me down. o, that's silly . . ."

"Oh? No, no, no, I would have welcomed you," says he who was once the world's most famous political prisoner.

"Oh, that's wonderful," trills she who doesn't even exist.

"Mr President, your memories of Christmas?"

Mandela remembers Christmas as a child. "The only time when we could have, in the countryside, sugar."

We spoke about this afterwards. Every white person within ear-shot was startled by this fact. We overweight, dieting blobs, to whom sugar is like kryptonite to Superman, hearing how sugar was Christmas for a small black kid in the Transkei. President Mandela gently rubs our noses into the sugar! "Because tea and coffee were reserved for elderly people, but at Christmas then they gave us, you know, some coffee and sugar. Some syrup, you know, with bread . . . "

"*Stroop en brood? Ja!*" agrees the *tannie* with the sweet tooth.

"Right!" confirms her President. "And then, of course, we would slaughter a sheep. That is what I remember . . ."

"Do you . . ." Evita starts, but he is not yet finished.

". . . and also seeing our mothers walking from house to house, village to village, kraal to kraal . . . er. . . eating almost the whole afternoon. I still remember those things."

Now was the chance to move to those twenty-seven years of limbo. "And in prison, did you ever have an opportunity to cele-brate Christmas?" Evita puts on her liberal face of drawn sympa-thy. Her voice becomes a whisper. "Was there a . . ." But he doesn't share her sense of tut-tuttage.

"Oh yes! We did, we really did! And they allowed us to buy a packet of sweets, a packet of fruits. That is what we enjoyed there. And then when some of us were in "A Group", you could buy a lot of goodies and enjoy Christmas."

"Oh, that's wonderful," applauds Mrs Bezuidenhout, delighted that her side had shown such compassion.

"And then, of course, we used to have games."

Evita ploughs on through the fields of good nature. "Do you have a chance now to enjoy laughter?" she asks as if his past was one big hoot. "Is there time to have a good time?"

"It is very difficult," he intones, losing the twinkle. "The programme is very tight." He goes on to explain how he has been allowed a half day of work, but how this in practice is quite impossible.

"And to relax?" That's something we all want to know. I beam out at him through Evita's eyes.

"Oh, the relaxation comes only in the morning. When I wake up every morning at five o'clock, I am on the road." Just to hear this makes my heart sink. How exposed he is every day to harm, and that only in his need to relax and keep fit! "For about an hour, sometimes a little more than an hour. But when I go home to my country village, I walk up to the distant villages and cross little rivers and climb hills and so on. Sometimes it takes about two, sometimes three, even sometimes five hours of just walking and talking to the people in the villages."

The twinkle is back. He is not faxing me a prepared statement. I remember the remarkable news that Nelson Mandela had built a holiday home near his village based on the design of the house in which he had stayed at the Vic Verster Prison. Like me and you, Evita also wants to know why.

"Could you explain to me why you chose that design?"

He takes in the question, purses his lips, nods slightly, narrows his eyes, then opens them wide, moving from ancient Mandarin to aged Griqua, takes a breath and articulates carefully.

"Well, you know, I stayed in that house from 1988 to 1990. I was all alone and I became friendly to the walls of that house. And it left a very formidable impression on me. And that is why I wanted to carry that impression with me to my country village. And because I had some of the most pleasant memories in that cottage in Victor Verster. That is where most of the negotiations with the top government team that was set up for this purpose took place and the decisions made about the future of South Africa. And so, that house in the country village represents those memories."

"Is it difficult to be the world's greatest hero?"

He looks grave. "I don't spend much time on that, because the world has many heroes. I myself have many heroes and my heroes are the men and women who have chosen to bring about happiness into the heart of everybody, whatever his background, whatever his race. And I am heartened by the fact that we are rich in such men and women in our own country."

"Your inspirations. Who were they?" Evita now asks, just dying to know what makes this extraordinary man tick. Again this puts Mandela into a collective mode.

"Well . . . er . . . it's not very easy to say that, because we are an organization which believes in a collective leadership. And . . . er . . . it is the collective effort of all South Africans, of all human beings that is important, not really an individual." He pauses. Evita hmmms. I wait. The seconds tick by. "There are many people that I admire for their courage or for their vision, for their foresight. And in this country, one man who had that vision was . . . er" He keeps us in suspense. Who will he mention? De Klerk? Pik? "Minister Kobie Coetsee."

Well, blow me down! The former Minister of Justice? Evita can only echo our amazement. "Wraggies, ja!"

"Because at a time when no member of the National Party wanted to hear about the ANC, that was the man who was working systematically with me to make it possible for the ANC and the government to sit down and to talk. And I have immense respect for that man."

"Well," says Evita Bezuidenhout, love pouring from every pore. "It's very easy to say that you are definitely **my** greatest hero!"

He breaks out into a wonderful all-embracing smile. "Well, that is mutual, because you are my hero!"

Time for the gift. "Mr President, I have a gift for you . . . " The box is scribbled full of changes of address. "It was sent to Robben Island . . ." there it stands: his name and number, scratched out to be sent to Pollsmoor. "There they sent it to the Vic Verster. Then I think someone sent it to Tuynhuis, Cape Town . . . Also scratched out! . . . but they wrote 'Return to Sender'!" This actually had happened to an important letter recently sent to the President at Tuynhuis. Returned to sender. Person unknown! Evita opens the box. There lies the red ethnic shirt with her face smiling out.

Mandela laughs, clearly delighted.

"A special shirt to remind you of this very special occasion."

"I'll value this," he tells her. "Thank you very much!"

On the inside of the box is the photo of Mevrou. She reads the written message to him. "For Madiba, Eternally yours. *Amandla! Vrystaat*! Evita Bezuidenhout."

Evita takes Nelson Mandela's hand and holds it. "I want to thank you for everything that you are doing for us and for being such a friend to us and for inspiring us with so much love and affection for the future."

"You are welcome," Nelson Mandela says. "You are very generous. You have done wonderful work too and we are proud of you. And I mean it when I say: you **are** one of my heroes!"

"That's it," I whisper. It is 29 minutes 47 seconds! The interview is over. Cut!

"I must quickly show you what I look like without the wig!" I whisper. The cameras are not present. Good. I don't want everything to look like a photo opportunity.

Nelson twinkles at me, nodding. I whip off Evita's wig. He gasps.

"Oh very good! Put it back on! I would never recognize you like that!"

We laugh and hug again. Our stills man catches us. He snaps two pics with me, wig in hand, with Nelson Mandela laughing. One of my favourite pics ever!

And then he was gone. Back to the world. Having left us with one of the most extraordinary thirty minutes of friendship.

# QUINTUS VAN DER MERWE

In 1998 I was privileged to meet President Mandela during the national celebration of Freedom Day in Cape Town. I was in charge of the VIP stage, and inter alia had to help arrange that nine children representing the nine provinces would walk onto the stage in front of the City Hall and shake the President's hand. To save costs I collected nine children from the vicinity and made each one wear a T-shirt from a different province. When my son, wearing a Northern Cape T-shirt, came forward, President Mandela asked him: "From where in the Northern Cape are you?" He looked quickly at me and answered: "No Sir, I am from Cape Town." Thereupon Mandela threw his arms in the air and said to everyone around him: "It's a fake, all these children are from the Cape!" He drew my son, who looked rather uncertain, closer and laughingly hugged him. He looked over at me, and winked.

# TONY LAVINE

When I first met Madiba in the early 1990s he shook my hand and said: "I will never wash this hand again". Of course, he never said this to anybody else . . . the old charmer. Ever since, I have tried to visualise him washing his left hand only!

Some time later, he was due at our house for dinner. Quite early that morning, two members of his guard detail – Mark and Jason, I think – turned up to check the security of our property. Not being morning people, we were not yet up and about so we asked our domestic worker to show them through to the pool area and make them coffee.

We had just acquired a very large German-bred Alsatian who had retired after a highly successful career as a police reservist. Since we were not yet quite as well trained as Nero, we didn't know what his reaction to strangers would be. So we closed him in a bedroom, not realising that the door was open onto a small courtyard with a chest-high wall.

Having been a top police dog, Nero picked up the scent of the security guys and obviously classified them as hostiles. He vaulted the courtyard wall with ease, assessed the situation in an instant and went into attack mode. He took a flying leap at the closest guard, knocking him into the pool – fortunately at the shallow end because it turned out that he couldn't swim. While he floundered around in shock, Nero instantly zeroed in on his companion, another big and fit guy as his position demanded. But it didn't help him. The powerful animal sunk his teeth into the guard's backside just below his flak jacket, bringing him down and putting him out of action. He had to be patched up in hospital.

Shortly afterwards, Nelson phoned to say that something had come up and he wouldn't be able to make dinner. On hearing what had taken place, he roared with laughter and said: "Tell you what, you keep Mark and Jason and I'll take the dog."

# WYNDHAM HARTLEY

I was part of the press corps when Mandela was visited by Chancellor Helmut Kohl. The President took the leader of a reunified Germany for a walk through the Tuynhuys garden. A photographer, Jean du Plessis, was walking backwards ahead of them to get a good shot of the two when he fell into the pond. Quick as a flash, Mandela moved to help him out, but fortunately some security guards got there first. "And that," Mr Mandela informed the German leader, "is our pool photographer!"

# ZAPIRO (JONATHAN SHAPIRO)

In 1997 Cape Town made a bid for the 2004 Olympic Games. On the night of the announcement of the host city, I was one of the thousands of people who gathered on the Parade in Cape Town. Many South Africans thought we stood a good chance. After all, we had Madiba Magic, it was post-apartheid and so why would we not get it? As we know it did not go quite the way we thought it would. There was a live TV link up from Switzerland and we watched in silence as they announced: "The host city for 2004 is: Athens!" There was total disbelief and a muttering of discontent went through the crowd. Suddenly my friend, the journalist Tony Weaver, who was standing next to me started laughing his head off. A person close to him had mumbled in typical Cape Town fashion: "Athens se ma se @£$%*!" "There is your cartoon," Tony said. At first I wasn't sure how I could use it, but a few days later I realised what to do. I depicted the Parade at night after the announcement, with no one there any more except this one disgruntled person saying: "Athens se ma se £$%*&". In a way he was representing the feeling of all South Africans. That cartoon became the most popular I had ever done. It just went crazy.

A few days after the cartoon appeared, Madiba arrived back from Switzerland where he was heading up our bid. He addressed the ANC caucus in parliament where everyone was very downhearted at having lost the bid. I was later told by ANC MPs that he said: "I didn't know what I was going to say and then I saw this," and he hauled out a copy of the Sowetan with my cartoon in it. He then read out: "Athens se ma se . . . MOER!" Apparently all the MPs just collapsed laughing. I thought it was brilliant! Although I was very relieved at the same time, that Madiba was not from Cape Town and did not quite know what the expletive actually was. At least the word "moer" is a bit softer than the typical Cape Town version.

# WARMTH

"I always knew
that deep down
in every human heart,
there is mercy
and generosity."

NELSON MANDELA

# DAVID BRADSHAW

Shortly before Nelson Mandela became president, I had flown from my home in Johannesburg to Durban to give a presentation to members of the travel trade. My back was giving me problems, so my local sales executive took me to her doctor straight from the airport. He gave me an injection and told me to go to the Royal Hotel where I was staying and rest before the evening function. I was then to be collected by my sales executive later that afternoon and taken to the event.

When it was time to get ready, I was so stiff that I could hardly move. I very slowly made my way downstairs to wait for her. Whilst standing in the middle of the reception area, the doors suddenly swung open and who should walk towards me but Nelson Mandela, with a group of men, presumably security. Afterwards I would feel a little embarrassed and disrespectful for not getting out of his way, but it happened so quickly and with my back so stiff, I was glued to the spot. Mr Mandela walked towards me whilst I thought he was much taller than I had imagined. Seeing me he walked over to me, gave me that beaming smile and then shook my hand. I think we both said good afternoon and then in a flash he was gone. It all happened so quickly and I stood there very surprised and very touched. Firstly it was so great to see him and secondly to receive such a warm greeting from such a great man who is admired by the whole world. I will treasure that handshake and brief moment forever.

# DERICK BRUMMER

I have an overt disability as a result of an accident that happened when I was going to a Grade VIII Drama lesson.

Years later, I was walking out of a shop when this man, who *kinda* looked like Nelson Mandela . . . but he also didn't look like I would have expected Madiba to look like . . . walked up to me! It's not something you expect to happen to you, especially not with an overt disability because people tend to steer clear of you.

Due to my history which was very drama-oriented I looked around for a camera (*a la* Candid Camera) but the only 2 people who I saw who were paying any attention to us were two rather hefty men in suits (who I take it were his bodyguards).

I didn't walk up to him . . . he walked up to **me** and shook **my** hand! No words were exchanged, apart from a "Hello" and a grin from Madiba, as I was too star-struck. I was basically overwhelmed, trying to take in the whole situation.

The memory will live with me forever.

# KEVIN
# CHAPLIN

The first time I met Nelson Mandela is a day I will never forget. It was at Archbishop Desmond Tutu and Mama Leah's 50th wedding anniversary in Soweto, Johannesburg.

My wife Robyn and I went up to take communion in the church and as we turned around to go back to our seats we ended up face to face with Madiba and the lovely Graca Machel. Well, it almost took our breath away. He could see our shock and smiled. He was to the side of the queue so we were able to stop and shake his hand and, of course Grace Machel's, and say how good it was to meet him and thank him for who he was. I was taken by the softness of his very large hands and there was most certainly an aura surrounding him. Even more so he was so humble about the compliments I was bestowing upon him. He seemed almost shy to be praised so highly. It truly felt a magical moment. My wife was radiant as we engaged briefly with him. We could not get outside the church afterwards fast enough in order to call our daughters and tell them about this amazing experience and how blessed we were. In fact, my wife's first words were: "You won't believe who we just met." What a highlight of our lives!

The second time I met this amazing man, I was sitting in the row behind him and Graca Machel in the church for Hlumelo Biko's wedding. I was one seat behind and to the right of him so I had an awesome opportunity to simply gaze at this remarkable human being who, for me, is the most powerful example of Ubuntu. Just having the opportunity to watch his facial expressions and see the impact of a human being on a nation was remarkable and inspiring. I again made sure I did not miss out on the opportunity to shake those soft, puffy hands and feel true greatness, even if for just a short time.

We were blessed a third time at Mamphela Ramphele's 60th birthday party. Robyn and I were able this time to really engage him and have a range of photos taken with him. What a privilege! We were in awe to be in his presence. We felt like nothing else mattered – just to be able to shake his hand again and chat with him. I can't recall exactly what we spoke about but he laughed out loud at something I said and it was so mesmerizing to experience this joy and to be in the presence yet again of such a humble and warm human being.

Being in his presence and engaging so briefly with him each time I learnt that true greatness starts within and Madiba's ability to connect with people and to make them feel so important is what a true leader is all about. The world is blessed to have had such a statesman in their midst.

# LINDA MORRIS

It was the 12th of July 1993. I had been on holiday in the States visiting friends and relatives with my two daughters Peta-Lynn who was 11 years old at the time and Gaby who was eight years old. We were flying home on flight SA 202 from New York Kennedy airport.

The plane was one of those big jumbos, which had a small economy section upstairs. We were fortunate to have seats there.

After dinner and watching movies, a lot of people were sleeping. Peta-Lynn and I were thirsty so we got up to go to the kitchen just behind us. Imagine our surprise when we saw Mandela in the kitchen! He was on his own, but I could see a bodyguard standing halfway up the stairs. He was stretching his legs getting some exercise.

He was so friendly and warm towards us. He greeted us and then offered to make us some tea! He said he was travelling with his daughters and with a school choir. He had just received the

Nobel Peace Prize in New York. He was so affable and interested in where we had been. He chatted to us like an old friend and I felt very comfortable with him. I tried to wake Gaby, but she was so fast asleep. She could kick herself now!

He let us take photos of each other with him and signed autographs.

It was a very special moment which we will treasure forever.

# PIET VAN ROOYEN

Some time in 1994 or 1995, I won the CNA beginner's prize for my novel *The Tracker* (*Die Spoorsnyer*). I was rather proud of this, because I had moved four or five years previously from the then peaceful South Africa to the unknown of a Namibia becoming independent, where everything was still very unsettled, precisely with the aim of becoming a so-called writer. Many things had happened in the meantime. South Africa had obtained majority rule, Nelson Mandela had been released from prison. He was ready to rule. There was a new country with new hope for a peaceful future.

I had just lived through the wonderful experience of penning down the life-story of a good friend and comrade, the Bushman tracker /Ui Chapman, and turning it into fiction. It was therefore with a considerable amount of satisfaction and contentment that I flew to Johannesburg to receive the prize.

Everything was rather overwhelming and hazy. Only here and

there did I look up to see properly. The prize-giving was in a neatly arranged hall somewhere between narrow streets and litter in a previously unsavoury part of the city. I had not realized that at the same event Nelson Mandela would receive the CNA prize for his autobiography *Long Walk to Freedom*. Only when the prize-winners were announced I heard his name, and realized in what company I was. He went up modestly to receive his prize, without much fanfare and without saying much more than "Thank you".

Shortly afterwards my name was called. I walked forward to the space in front where the lights were shining and the winners' envelopes were handed over. The hall was packed with guests, but I could only see them dimly in the semi-darkness of the hall with the bright lights in front. I received my prize and walked back to my seat to the sound of applause. I am rather retiring or shy by nature and apprehensive of too many people in a crowd. My head was therefore hanging a bit as I walked back.

Suddenly the clapping stopped. The hall gasped. The deathly silence made me look up. Slightly behind me, in a seat I had already passed, in the second row, stood Nelson Mandela, his hand extended in a gesture of congratulation. The grey head and broad smile were clearly visible in the dusk of the darkened hall.

I silently cursed my inattention. But fortunately it was not too late. I turned around and went to shake his hand. "Congratulations!" he said softly, the broad smile still on his face. The crowd let out its breath and started clapping again.

This is a great man, I realized. It was with a sense of satisfaction and hope for the future of South Africa that I could return to my own country. With someone like him at the helm the future looked bright.

# SHIREEN HUSAIN

My dad's brother was a member of the SA Communist Party in the early 60's. The ANC was banned and Madiba was on the run from the Security Branch. While he was in hiding he stayed in Kinross, Mpumalanga at my uncle's house, while en route to Swaziland.

I also attended his 75th birthday party. There is no question about the charisma he exuded. Each guest was given a little beaded Zulu doll. Both dolls we received enjoy pride of place on our mantlepiece. I always remind my children where the dolls came from so that they appreciate them as a piece of history.

In 1988, through my husband's involvement with the SA Law Society, I had the privilege to shake his hand and he was exceptionally warm with my daughter who was 2 at the time. His warmth and love for children was very obvious.

# VICKY MEREDITH

I am a secondary school teacher working in Dublin. In August 2011 I was lucky enough to meet Nelson Mandela at his home in Qunu with a group of eight other Irish Teachers.

We had travelled in July 2011 to the Eastern Cape with an education NGO called Link Community Development, of which Archbishop Desmond Tutu is patron. We each worked in a junior secondary school in separate local communities between Mveso and iDutywa. One weekend we were travelling to Coffee Bay to discuss what we had been doing in our respective schools and to plan a workshop for teachers in that district. We stopped at the gates of Nelson Mandela's house in Qunu as he was still there after visiting for his birthday. As the final group got ready to continue on their journey they met Mandela's grandson, Mandla Mandela, on his way in. He was very curious about what we were doing in Eastern Cape, and surprised that we were staying in the rural communities.

He invited us to Mveso on International Women's Day where we participated in the Women's ANC celebrations for 'Women's Day', ate dinner with the community and Mandla gave us a tour of the development projects in the village. Then he invited us to his grandfather's house for dinner on the Friday, which was to be our last day with our schools. I was very taken aback that he would be willing to do that for us.

We travelled to the house at Qunu and when Mandla arrived he brought us straight into the house to the dining room where Nelson Mandela was sitting at the head of the dining room table. We all shook hands with him, said hello in our Xhosa and his grandson spoke a little to him about who we were. Madiba was in bad health and did not speak to us other than to say hello. However, when a childhood friend, who we were told often kept him company when he was there, joined us, Mr Mandela spoke in Xhosa and everybody who spoke Xhosa was soon laughing since there was a very warm and humorous exchange between the two.

I am sure that we were quite a picture as several of us were dressed in Xhosa clothing with traditional beads that our schools had presented to us as gifts. The teachers in my school had packed away my regular clothes and sent them home with my house-mother so that I would be in traditional clothing complete with locally made shoes when I met him. Mandla offered to take a photo for us and Mr Mandela agreed. (Since I came home it has been on my classroom wall and all of my students hear how lucky we were.)

I was the last one of our group to leave the dining room and when I got to the door I turned to smile and wave at Mr Mandela. He smiled and gave me a small wave. His warmth and dignity were very apparent and that moment is a treasured memory.

We spent only a few minutes in his company. It was a true honour to be welcomed into his home, especially when he was in poor health. We had been welcomed into our Eastern Cape communities with warmth and openness, treated with great care and been very well looked after, it had already been an exceptional experience. Little did we know as we enjoyed the significance of standing outside his home while he was there that three weeks later we would be so generously welcomed inside without pomp or ceremony, himself and his family giving us an incredible opportunity to meet an incredible man and spend a few treasured minutes in his company. And of course for me to share a smile was wonderful.

# ZAPIRO (JONATHAN SHAPIRO)

In 1994, my wife Karina, who is a photographer, was working on a documentary about Madiba. She of course got to meet him and spent a lot of time with him. A few months later we heard someone was putting together a photographic book: *A day in the life of the new South Africa* and Karina organised a shoot through Madiba's office. I immediately said to her: "Of course you'll need an assistant." She said: "Sure, but on the precondition that you don't say who you are, since it might be a distraction." My cartoons were already appearing then in numerous South African newspapers. So I tagged along and got introduced as "Jonathan." I am the most irreligious person, but for me meeting Madiba was the closest I had come to having a religious experience – the charisma, the warmth, the aura that he had and the way he really made you feel you were the only person in the world for that moment. I have never experienced anything like that before or since. We had about 20 minutes while Karina was doing the shoot and then she said to Madiba: "My husband here is actually Zapiro the cartoonist." Madiba's face lit up and he said: "Ah, Zapiro," in that lovely warm tone that he had. "I am really glad to meet you." It turned out that he knew not only my cartoons that had been published in the papers since his release, but he knew my work even from when he was in prison. He had seen drawings of mine from years back and knew where I was coming from politically which was fantastic. I was thrilled by how much he seemed to value and enjoy the cartoons.

# REFERENCES

*Cape Times*, 13 December 2013: Peter Storey p 187.

*Huffington Post*, 8 December 2013: Meredith Carlson Daly p 58.

*Sunday Times* supplement, 8 December 2013: Ahmed Kathrada p 67, 75, 81, 240; Richard Stengel p 77; Rory Steyn p 127; Sally Rowney p 147; Johnny Clegg p 294; Bruce Fordyce p 319.

*Daily Dispatch*, 8 December 2013: Fumbatile Mbilini in conversation with Mpumzi Zuzile p 141.

*Independent Newspapers* memorial edition, December 2013: Jakes Gerwel p 68.

*The Observer*, 8 June 2008: Zelda La Grange (interview with John Carlin) p 194.

*The Independent*, 15 December 2013: Shanti Aboobaker p 285.

**Do you have a story about meeting Nelson Mandela? Please send it to mandelastories@gmail.com for future editions.**